If I Catch You I Will Kill You

A Childhood Sexual Abuse Survivor Redefines Life On Her Own Terms

JUDY FERRARO

ISBN-13: 978-1492909941
ISBN-10: 1492909947

DEDICATION

I dedicate this book to Oprah Winfrey who tirelessly brought to light the topic of sexual abuse in children and the consequences experienced by the victims. Never did she waiver on her quest to bring healing to those who have suffered from the effects of childhood molestation.

And to Mackenzie Phillips who, after her own segment on "The Oprah Winfrey Show," catapulted me from a treadmill to my laptop to begin writing my own story of childhood abuse. I understand you, Mackenzie, and want you to know how much you inspired me to move forward in my healing process.

CONTENTS

FORWARD

Don't worry. When you read this book, you will find that I never did kill anyone. But you will experience how rage trumped fear, how support inspires those who are fragile, and the power of Pine-Sol®.

My story is about finding comfort, recognizing support, trusting your instincts, overcoming adversity and finding peace. I am already joyful. Even before being published, this book became a catalyst to inform and heal.

It is my intent to reach parents, teachers, aunts, uncles, cousins, clergy, neighbors and friends of all children in an effort to protect the young from sexual abuse. It is our job to teach children to communicate, observe their behaviors, and immediately respect their cries for help. Parents must explain to children early and often what types of touching are appropriate and inappropriate, making sure the child understands their words.

And in the end, I began a new journey. That of forgiveness. Forgiving my abuser sets me free. It is not the unconditional forgiveness we exchange with our parents or friends, but one that calms the anger that festered in my heart and mind for decades. It is now my time for peace.

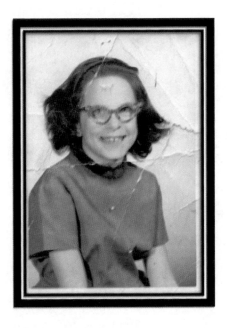

Hiding behind my glasses in perhaps my most unattractive photo.

1 THE DOMINO EFFECT

I suffer from anxiety, just like so many of the others. Ask any sexual abuse survivor. The fallout comes when it's least expected. Like a chain reaction, one small incident can lead to a breakdown that lasts for months simply by toppling over the first domino.

No matter how much therapy, how many life changes, or how much time has elapsed, the fallout from sexual abuse changes the way you live your life. The aftermath follows its survivors into every corner of our lives and affects our relationships with friends, relatives, our dates and spouses, our coworkers and the children we love.

With every disaster there is an aftermath. And sexual abuse is a disaster. We never know when a memory is going to creep up on us. Just when we think we are afloat, a hand emerges from the water and pulls us under. There are triggers that take us back.

Something in the news. A book or magazine article. Even a casual conversation with someone who does not know about my sexual abuse. No one knew — I didn't tell — until now. The triggers for me can be as simple as a face like that of my abuser, a hairline, a freckle, a smile. Soft sexual conversation disconnects me. Certain kinds of touching sends me tumbling into my own private abyss. I find it painful to watch movies with victims of any type. I cower as they cower. I close my eyes, leave the theater or turn the channel. I cannot be taken back. That's undoubtedly the fallout of sexual abuse. It is difficult to tell the difference between fiction and reality. And like a virus, each reminder has to run its course.

Learning of the Elizabeth Smart or Jaycee Dugard nightmare takes me back to my awful place. They were abused over and over, to the point of believing that the abuse was normal. The thought of being held prisoner sends me into a spin. For so long, I was a prisoner being held hostage by my inability to ask for help.

Self-esteem is damaged, sometimes beyond repair. For some survivors of abuse, the damage is so deep that a journey to normalcy is too difficult. They deal with their horrid pasts alone and without answers or support. Obesity, promiscuity, multiple marriages, trust issues — the list goes on and on. I lived my life never feeling beautiful, inside or out. I always felt that I was bad. I looked in the mirror and saw nothing. Rather than thinking about my looks, I performed comedy, sang and danced my way into the hearts of those whose love I wanted. Performing helped me feel less invisible.

Invisible is how one feels while being abused. Why doesn't someone care? Why doesn't someone see how frightened I am? Why doesn't anyone notice? Why do they look at me, knowing that I'm different or odd, and not explore why? Many victims block out the entire experience, but still carry the behaviors and scars created by sexual abuse.

In my case, I always wanted to be the center of attention. In middle school classrooms, I talked incessantly and found myself in trouble with the teachers despite my good grades. I started to swear, for surely that would make me appear cool.

Like many teenage girls, I earned cash by babysitting. Afterward, I would be subjected to being alone with the fathers of the children. They were often a little tipsy and would drive or walk me home. I never felt safe. I worried that they would try to touch me. I remember running into my house, locking the door and leaning on it, feeling as if I had just escaped something terrible.

As I got older, around high school age, the anxiety lessened and then vanished. Without the anxiety, I began to connect with others. There were wonderful teachers and administrators at my schools who began to tap into my talents. I was no longer invisible. High school was a good time in my life. I was free. I developed friendships that I cherish to this day. I could have been a better student — I had the brains for it — but instead I concentrated on having fun. It was my first shot at happiness. I was a pompom girl and hung with a crazy group of girls who thought it was fun to enjoy Boone's Farm wine or Jim Beam in our McDonald's diet cola. I was funny and stopped wearing my glasses, opting for a try at being pretty even if I couldn't see.

In my 20s, while working and going to night school, most of my romances were brief, including my first marriage. I was incapable of trusting and felt that men were using me. This is an example of the fallout. Sexually, I was messed up. Little did I know that I would never have a functional relationship without therapy. My second husband Michael and I have been married for nearly two decades and have a son. He is in college now, but there was always the worry that he might endure something as painful and shameful as I had. We have a good marriage in spite of his support for the Cubs and mine of the White Sox.

Our union has lasted due to the couple's therapy we sought before getting married. I know there are times when my abuse affects our relationship. I often stumble then regroup to find my footing. Michael doesn't ask many questions. Perhaps he doesn't want to cause me pain; maybe the conversation is painful for him. While writing this book I find it is important to get back to counseling and find out why.

Even after all this time, rearing my own child has been a challenge due to my abuse fallout. He is a teenager now, but there is always the worry that he might endure something as painful and shameful as I had. I taught him at a young age what was appropriate and inappropriate. Most importantly, I taught him to communicate freely with his father and me about anything, anytime. I still find it difficult to trust unsupervised males in his presence. When he was younger, I kept him away from situations where he would be alone with coaches, teachers and priests. I treaded lightly and rarely left him at the home of a friend when the mother was out. I avoided summer camps. I had long talks with him about what was the right kind of touching and the wrong kind of touching before ever leaving him with a babysitter. And when we did have a babysitter, I asked questions, lots of them, about their time together. I made sure that as an only child, he built strong and comfortable relationships with his aunts, uncles, cousins and family friends. Never did I want him to feel the pain of not knowing what to do. This type of caretaking never goes away.

I was worried about how he might receive this book. We survivors never stop thinking about how our experience may hurt others. We are always in the protection mode.

I also feel the need to protect other children. I've talked to my nieces about inappropriate advances and touching. And I find myself having that discussion with many of the young girls that I love. It is what I do. It is because I wish someone had thought to have that conversation with me — had given me a green light to share any and all information. Even though I had myriad people to lean on in my early life, I didn't know that I could ask for help. I didn't know that sharing would be healing. I didn't know that the anger wouldn't be directed at me. I didn't know how or when to begin the healing process.

I invite you now, on my journey of healing. The path I chose was that of an obstacle course. Highs, lows, walls and falls. There are better ways. I wish that it were easier. And that longing for guidance remains.

Me in 1ˢᵗ grade with my fairy glasses and black tooth.

2 WHY NOW?

From the Bible, Ecclesiastes III

> 3:1 To everything there is a season, and a time
> to every purpose under the heaven:
>
> 3:2 A time to be born, and a time to die; a time
> to plant, and a time to pluck up that
> which is planted;

3:3 A time to kill, and a time to heal; a time to break down, and a time to build up;

3:4 A time to weep, and a time to laugh; a time to mourn, and a time to dance;

3:5 A time to cast away stones, and a time to gather stones together; a time to embrace, and a time to refrain from embracing;

3:6 A time to get, and a time to lose; a time to keep, and a time to cast away;

3:7 A time to rend, and a time to sew; a time to keep silence, and a time to speak;

3:8 A time to love, and a time to hate; a time of war, and a time of peace

There simply is a season that applies to every event in our lives. Though I am not able to eloquently quote the Bible, I do think about my own journey when I hear this passage. There was a time I kept silent and a time that I spoke. There is a difference between speaking to respond and speaking to be heard. After nearly five decades of silence followed by denial, it is my time to be heard.

Trudging through life with a dark secret isn't easy,

especially if it starts when you are very young. Can you remember the last time you asked a 5-year-old to keep a secret? Inevitably, the child bursts with just the thought of sharing a secret. But the game changes when the secrets are your own shameful, private and carefully concealed pieces of information. I lived the secret for decades.

On my first day of school I was sure my classmates could see that I had a secret, just by looking at me. Surely the boys knew there was something wrong with me. I chewed my nails to a nub, sucked my thumb at night and picked my nose in private. I was good at hiding things.

While gracefully surfing my own personal and seemingly eternal wave of denial, I was and am constantly reminded of my secret. The Penn State saga. Every priest gone bad. The boring homilies written to address "the pedophile issue" in an effort to heal the Catholics. Every talk show host who interviews sexual abuse victims. Every child who has gone missing. Every famous person who shares a story of abuse. The Internet. Every inappropriate touch or look from a male teacher, coworker or friend. A face similar to my abuser's. They can all bring the horror back. I am always watching and suspecting. Almost daily, something can throw me — even if only for a moment — to a deep, dark place.

My tendency to distrust others has followed me throughout my entire life. I find it difficult to forgive cheaters, people who tell lies, and those who personally and professionally use other people. Mountains of energy are expended when living in fear and distrust. It's exhausting. There were times when I could have reached the point of reconciliation with others sooner. But when I'm wronged by someone I care for, forgiveness is difficult. Heinous betrayal of a child's trust teaches the victim that to be liked, loved or trusted, the sexual abuse must be endured. Therapists explain that this may create a lasting tolerance or even a need for hurt and humiliation. Childhood survivors often grow up helpless and confused about what is safe, what is to be trusted and who protects. What is reality? What is imagination? And what is fact?

All too often, the Catholic Church — where I built my relationship with God — torments me with a "priest molests children" report. Recently, it was a priest who molested over 200 children at a school for the deaf. Those children were perfect victims, vulnerable in many ways. The priest is dead and gone and the deaf victims are "speaking out." It is their time; it is their season. The Pope is trying to fix the problem. Too little, too late is how I see it.

And almost daily, I can count on a news story that pushes me down to that dark place. Every young girl found raped and murdered, offenders pleading not guilty, and DNA tests that free the wrongfully convicted are reminders.

***

When I was 6 years old, a breaking news story accompanied a photo of a girl about my age with sparkly fairy glasses similar to my own. She had gone missing. I watched as her mother pleaded for the return of her precious little girl on the evening news. I knew her abductor was a man and I knew what he was doing to her and I knew if she told, he would kill her.

The little girl was found unclothed and dead in a forest preserve a few days later. The news coverage said she had been raped. I didn't know what that meant, but I knew he had touched her, the same way that someone was touching me. And rather than risk being caught, he just killed her. I was glad that I was alive and not left dead beneath a tree. I was never going to tell.

That is, until watching an Oprah show in 2009, some 34 years later. I had watched a number of Oprah segments that discussed sexual abuse. But for some reason, Mackenzie Phillips' story stirred me into action. Her experience was horrific. I cried for Mackenzie and her stolen innocence. Even though she knew the abuse was wrong, she still somehow trusted her father and mourned his death. I understood her sadness.

When discussing Mackenzie's story with others, I found that my interpretation of it was different from theirs. I thought everyone would feel badly for her, as I had. Surely people would know that sharing her story was part of her healing process. The reaction from most was that they believed her, but asked "Why now?" Was it for attention? Would she gain financially by opening up on a talk show? Perhaps book sales? Some even indicated that it seemed she enjoyed the sex. I couldn't believe my ears. They didn't and couldn't understand. She wrote her book to reach out to others who may be suffering. Maybe Mackenzie would give them the courage to take the necessary step to begin their own healing.

Someone who has been victimized can understand. It's no secret that conversations about sexual abuse make most people feel uncomfortable. So we, the survivors, accommodate them and we keep our silence. And while we protect those who may feel uncomfortable with our pain, the abuser is also protected. It was Mackenzie's time; it was her season. It was her time to mourn and her time to find peace.

The catalyst for my book, was the follow-up segment about the Mackenzie Phillips book. I was exercising my older and less resilient body on my treadmill. Mackenzie wasn't a guest on the show, only the angry naysayers who showed disbelief in her story. In agitation, I increased the treadmill's speed, then the incline. But exercise was not going to dissipate my anger. I wiped my head and neck, turned off the treadmill and leaped up the basement stairs and straight to my laptop where I began to pound away at the keyboard. I sent an email canceling an appointment and all day long I poured my emotions into Microsoft Word. I was thankful for the computer because all I had to say would have been impossible to write by hand. My brain was moving faster than my fingers. I didn't go to work that day. I missed my hair appointment without canceling. I became oblivious to the world around me. I had something far more important to do.

And just like Mackenzie and anyone else who has waited, it was my time to speak. So for those of you who ask "Why now?" I say "Why not?" This message must get out. It is my season.

JUDY FERRARO

My siblings and me from left: me, Spike, Jeanette and Jean.

3 MY FAMILY

The common denominator among all sexual abuse survivors is one decision: the decision to speak or not to speak. The decision to tell can be immediate or it may take years. Or perhaps the sexual abuse remains hidden for all time. But if and when we begin to talk, we realize that something very special was taken from us.

Sexual abuse comes in all shapes and colors and once it happens, the damage can last a lifetime. When the child used to satisfy sexual desire doesn't tell, the conspiracy commences. The ugly secret is planted and sprouts like an invasive weed, over and over again. Innocence leaves and the betrayals begin.

There is so much I do not remember about my childhood. My siblings have vivid recollections of our family and childhood experiences. As I listen to them reminisce, I can't imagine how we grew up in the same house. Their stories are full of happy memories and they have a strong connection to the home in which we were raised. One sister still lives in the home that housed my nightmare. I am disconnected from that home in Midlothian, a southwest suburb of Chicago, and my sibling's stories.

Even though I didn't tell anyone about the abuse at the time, I felt betrayed by my parents for not protecting me. If only they had noticed that something was amiss. If only my older sister had watched out for me. If only I'd had the guts to tell someone. It wasn't like I didn't have close relationships. Once I learned to dial the telephone, I called my grandmother every day. Certainly I could have told her. I had friends at school and church. I spent time with wonderful teachers, neighbors, aunts and uncles. I could have told anyone. I am disappointed in myself. The betrayal began with my not telling. Why did I choose to endure the abuse alone? Why did I think that telling would make me the bad guy?

Why was I so afraid? These questions are in the minds of most child abuse victims.

***

By the time I was 3, I was diagnosed with a lazy eye and far sightedness that were corrected with blue sparkly glasses. I wore my glasses from the moment I woke up until I went to bed. They corrected not only my vision, they corrected my appearance and that of the world around me. With the glasses on, my eye stopped wandering and I could see the world in single rather than double vision. The glasses became a security blanket. The thought of losing or breaking them sent me into a panic. My glasses were initially my comfort, but when the sexual abuse began, they became my disguise.

To make matters worse, when I was 4, I tripped, fell into a cabinet and blackened my front baby tooth. I learned to smirk rather than smile to hide my ugly tooth. My ears were like wings protruding from my face and I insisted on putting my hair behind them to prevent the Dumbo flaps from peeking through the strands of my stringy black hair. I started avoiding the mirror because I knew I wasn't as pretty as other girls my age.

Like many victims, my self-esteem was damaged before the abuse began. That's what makes certain children easy targets. The predator knows which children to touch and which children not to touch. I was blind to anything positive about myself. Even if someone had complimented me, I wouldn't have heard them. I knew I was different. For my entire childhood, I felt less loved. I realize now I wasn't loved less; it just felt that way then.

I am the second child of four. My older sister enjoyed the "oldest" title; my brother was the "only boy;" and my younger sister was "the baby." I remember wanting to be someone — have a title of sorts — but there wasn't one for me. "Middle girl" just didn't sound as special as the other labels. My parents didn't use the labels; they were my own. I never quite felt as special as my siblings.

I was raised in a good family, in a blue-collar suburb. My mother was attentive and caring. My father was very funny and smart. He could fix anything. On weekends, our family enjoyed picnics at the nearby forest preserve. We took family road trips where we imposed upon relatives who lived in other states. We spent time on the waterways of Chicago in a boat my father purchased with credit union savings. We had family dinners every afternoon at 4:00. We laughed, sang, danced and loved. We were a nice family.

My older sister Jeanette was the family beauty. She is six years older than I am. She was the first child, the first grandchild and the first niece. She had what many of the "firsts" enjoy — no competition. In second grade I brought her to my classroom for show and tell. She adorned her Girl

Scout uniform with a sash of badges. I told my class how and why she had earned each badge. I remember her beaming as she stood in front of my class.

I was very happy when I was nearly 3 years old and my brother, Joseph Jr., (nicknamed Spike) was born. He and I formed a strong bond. I played with his trucks and he played with my dolls. Spike was cute and funny. I protected him in grade school, tortured him in high school, and in our 20s, we shared a rented apartment. I let him move in because he had a microwave and a chair. I am the godmother of his first child; he is the godfather of my son. We are close.

My younger sister came along when I was 6 years old. It concerned me that my mother had to go to a hospital to get her. My mom allowed us to pick the baby's name. We wanted to call her Jean, which is very similar to Jeanette. But the choice was ours, so Jean it was. When Jean came home, she became a live doll for Jeanette and me. We changed her outfits and styled her hair several times a day. Because of the 6-year age difference while growing up, Jean and I were worlds apart. We shared a room, but the age disparity meant different interests and different friends. The distance diminished as we got older. I liked watching out for Jean. She even married a man that I introduced to her. She is happy. Mission accomplished.

My mother was a stay-at-home mom who never got her

driver's license. This meant that we walked or rode our bicycles everywhere. She was supportive of her children, even when we were wrong. She was instantly loved by everyone. She was warm and patient. She loved to drink coffee with the neighbor ladies and tried to bring in an income by selling Avon, Beeline Clothing and Shaklee Vitamins.

My father was a TV repairman and owned a TV repair business that serviced commercial and residential accounts. He carried a case loaded with tubes and testers and diagnosed what was wrong with a TV right on the spot.

Some of my dad's large accounts were the motels along a stretch of highway west of Chicago called Route 45 or Mannheim Road. They were booming businesses before the expressways were built. Jeanette and I would go with our dad to his motel clients and while he was fixing the televisions, we swam in the pools. In the eyes of his children, it was the greatest job on earth, especially in the heat of the summer. Eventually, the highway expansions squelched the motels and my dad's livelihood. He was very sad when he lost his business, but I looked on the bright side. We had gained a bonus "sister."

At one of the motels, there was a young girl working as a maid making beds and cleaning rooms. My parents wondered why this 13-year-old blonde girl, Terry, was working so hard at such a young age. They asked the owners about her and were told that her mother was an alcoholic and hadn't heard much about her father. My parents asked her to babysit for our family occasionally, and by the time I was 4, she was living with us. Her mother didn't care that she spent time with our family and Terry was happy; she loved being with us. We ate dinner together every night. We watched Lassie, Bonanza and tuned into American Bandstand every Saturday and danced like the teenagers on TV. She was experiencing all the family traditions she had longed for and my parents had gained a babysitter. When we went on vacation, she came with us. On Christmas, she was visited by Santa just like the rest of us. He knew she was with us and not her mother. She had become our sister and brought a wonderful energy to our lives with her slightly teased blonde hair, gullible personality and bright smile. Life was good.

I especially loved Terry. She was exactly 10 years older than I was and provided the special attention I had always desired from Jeanette. She treated me as if I were her sister. She had fun teaching me pop songs and dancing the Twist. I came to cherish Terry and loved our close relationship. She and I shared a twin bed in the smallest room of the house.

Terry made friends in our neighborhood. A 15-year-old boy named Gil lived down the street and had a crush on her. Gil had red hair and freckles. He seemed so tall compared to my 4-year-old frame. He went to the local high school and had lots of friends. He was athletic, funny and entertaining. I can remember Gil and his friends very clearly. They all dressed alike in white tee shirts and jeans and they spent time working on cars — and even more time on their hair. They all smoked cigarettes. Gil often was in trouble with his parents, mostly his crabby stepfather. My mom became like a second mom to him.

Gil started spending lots of time at our home with Terry. My mother became close friends with his mother, a neighbor lady I loved, Mrs. Zampari. My father went fishing with his stepfather. From the day my brother could walk, he followed Gil as if he were the Pied Piper and mimicked his every move. The relationships with our families grew deep and strong. We liked when Gil came to our house. He was witty, helpful and charismatic. Terry loved him and so did I.

I remember thinking that Terry and Gil were in love. I would catch them kissing when my parents weren't around. When she was babysitting, I would watch him touch her in places that I had never seen anyone touched before. I remember him lying on top of her and moving around. They would moan and breathe hard. I didn't know what he was doing, but she didn't scream or act like she was being crushed. She even seemed to like it. And that was good enough for me. Sometimes I would jump on top of Gil and move the same way. It was fun.

Unfortunately, every few months, Terry's alcoholic mother would drive from the northwest side of Chicago to the southwest suburbs to snatch her away from us. Sometimes she showed up drunk in the middle of the night. When the welfare people were going to pay her a visit, she needed her daughter present in order to receive the check. We always knew that she would bring Terry back after she had been approved for her monthly stipend. I remember Terry leaving with her mother. I was concerned that her clothes and coat had been left behind. She needed her coat. She needed her shoes. Both my mother and Terry cried, hugging as she was torn away from us. I will never forget those traumatic departures. I don't know why my parents didn't just call the police. Maybe it is from our families that we victims learn "not to tell."

JUDY FERRARO

2ⁿᵈ grade, I picked those glasses to match my only dress.

4 THE ABUSE BEGINS

When Terry was with her mother, my parents often asked Gil to babysit. I was only 5 years old the first time Gil crawled into my twin bed. I could feel his warm breath on the back of my neck. He gently rubbed my back, first on the top of my pajamas and then his hand slid under the puckered flowered fabric. It felt good and sent me into a deep sleep. Later, falling into a deep slumber would be how I coped with his advances.

When Gil touched me, I lay still and unresponsive. My lifeless body was like a possum playing dead in hopes that its attacker would retreat. In retrospect, I thought that if I pretended to be sleeping, then I could make believe it wasn't happening. If my eyes were closed, surely Gil would think that I was asleep and that I would not remember what happened the next day. Thus, the next day, we could all be normal. I could like Gil just like everyone else did.

I'm not sure how many times I was abused between the ages of 5 and 10. My mind will not allow me to tally the number. My parents didn't have the funds to go out that often. But the occasional bowling banquet, Fireman's Ball or VFW dance would be their chance for some adult time with their friends, having some fun. Even when my sister was old enough to babysit, I remember that Gil was around. It seemed like he was always there.

Whether the abuse happened once or 100 times doesn't matter. Just like a car accident, the damage was done with the initial impact. His need to touch and rub up against me to satisfy his sick sexual impulses and invade my innocence changed me and influenced my behavior forever.

I know now that the first night Gil crept into my bed when I was 5, my childhood changed. More than changed — it was that night my childhood ended. My entire life was altered. I was no longer the fun-loving middle girl with blue glittery fairy glasses, big ears and a black front tooth. I had a secret, an adult secret. By night, when my glasses were off, I was a child living in fear. In the morning, I would carefully put on my glasses and carry on. Although my overall feeling was that of helplessness, I did my best to be a perfect daughter and sister, and I became very good at it.

My mother was very adept at making people like Terry and Gil feel like they were part of our family. She made it her business to reach out to the stragglers and misfits. She made them feel like they belonged. Because of her kindness and warmth, our small home was always open. Gil went from the red-haired freckled boy who babysat for us, to the teenager and then adult who hung out with his own friends at our house. I remember feeling panicky and wondering if his friends were going to touch me too. Relatives and neighbors raved about my mother's kindness and how she opened her home to all who needed one. But as I grew older, I wondered why she couldn't let our family just be the six of us. Why were there always others living in our family's 900-square-foot, one-bathroom home? From time to time, Gil would fight with his stepfather and be invited to stay on our couch for a few nights. I hated the thought of him being there. He was constantly granted access to me.

Gil's popularity soared to rock star status one summer morning because he called the ambulance when my mother began hemorrhaging on the kitchen floor. She hadn't known she was pregnant. The blood rushed down her leg onto the blue and white checkered tile floor. She was unconscious and losing lots of blood. She was miscarrying, and I thought she was dying. I don't recall who else was there at that moment; I just remember my mother being taken from us in an ambulance. My father was a volunteer fireman so we all knew the men who took her away. The siren blared and the lights flickered. She seemed safe with the men who were sent to save her. Gil received accolades for being there, all cool and collected. He had helped my mother. I remember thinking that maybe he had saved her life. Thank God for Gil.

By the time I was 6 he had free reign. The fondling transformed into a ritual of him rubbing and thrusting his crotch up against me again and again, until he groaned and finally stopped. In the beginning, he approached me from behind. On other occasions, as I grew older, he turned my limp body over and lay on top of me and moving around as he did with Terry. I remember feeling funny and tingly. He touched my undeveloped breasts, pinched at my tiny nipples. I recall touching myself to recreate the sensation.

I remember innocently telling my friends about the funny, tingly feeling and showing them how to make it happen. They were intrigued. At only 7, I was experiencing what I now know were orgasms from his rubbing, humping and touching me. He insisted I not tell anyone or else I would get in trouble. This was when I identified that what we were doing was wrong. Perhaps I was to blame. Maybe it was my fault after all.

Like most child abuse survivors, I believed that the evil things happened because I was innately bad. Self-blame runs rampant and revenge fantasies are common among us.

I often wonder what those childhood friends thought of me. I never did tell them where I learned how to get that feeling. They probably remember me as the perverted little girl from grade school. I shared with them the touching and rubbing motions I had learned. I'm sure as they matured, they might have looked back and wondered if I had become a lesbian.

As I grew older, I began to understand what was not appropriate. But as my family became closer to Gil and his family, I drifted further and further from ever being able to share my dark and dirty secret. Who would believe me? I was sure that everyone would be mad at me. If I told on Gil, who would my brother follow around? They would ask why I waited so long to tell. Maybe they wouldn't even believe me. That is the fear of every victim of child molestation. And after the fear comes the shame of it all.

When I was between the ages of 6 and 11, Terry came and went. Every time she returned, she was different. Her clothes smelled of smoke and often I caught a glimpse of her and Gil sneaking into the backyard to smoke Winston cigarettes. Those were the cigarettes that likely caused a stroke when she was in her late 40s. She lived the rest of her life in a nursing home.

They stood where no one could see them, smoking and laughing. Sometimes they kissed. Terry dropped out of high school and her life became erratic, like her mother's. She bounced between her mother's apartment and our home. Her departures became tearless since we had gotten used to them. I think she missed our family while she was with her mother. No matter how long she was away, I was always glad to see her return. When she was there, Gil didn't touch me. I loved her. And she, unknowingly, was my protector.

Gil swaggered off to join the Army when I was 10. There was a tragic war in Vietnam. American soldiers were dying. I was happy to see him leave, while others in my family talked of how they would miss him. I wished he would never return. He and Terry were now both gone. The smoke was gone; the sex was gone; and there was more room for us, just our family.

Occasionally, Gil came home on leave and headed straight to our house to visit my family. He looked handsome in his uniform and the neighborhood was proud of him for enlisting. Everyone would hug and kiss him and gather around to hear about his new life in the military. A hero's welcome. At just the thought of his arrival, and then when I saw his face, I would begin to worry that he would find a way to get me alone. And one day he did.

JUDY FERRARO

*The fateful day when I stood up to my abuser. This photo was
developed years after Gil took it.*

5 PINE-SOL®

By the age of 12, I was given the responsibility to clean the
house while my older sister drove my mother to the grocery
store and other weekly errands. It was Cinderella-esque. I was
left at home to clean while my sister was at the ball.

One Saturday morning, I was scrubbing the kitchen floor
on my hands and knees. Gil, who was home on leave from

the Army, entered the kitchen. I was wearing a very stylish and tight pair of maroon hip huggers. They were probably a size too small and I remember having to zip them by lying on my back. The zipper was only two inches long. While bending over to clean the floor, I am sad to admit, it was difficult to conceal my plumber's crack.

Gil stood around talking for a while, watching me clean the floor. I wasn't frightened of him anymore and found his presence to be annoying. I pulled my short, striped shirt down as far as I could. He spoke and I kept cleaning, nodding as he told me about his Army life. He talked about pushups and getting fit. He asked about Terry. Had I seen her lately? He kept watching me. I could feel his eyes following my every move. My body had developed a bit since he left, and I was self-conscious of those changes. I tried pulling my tight pants up to cover the top of my butt, but they were up as far as they would go. They were hip huggers, after all. I again tugged my shirt down to cover my bare midriff. I was uncomfortable.

I crawled to the far corner, my back against the wall, still cleaning. I kept my head down, trying to ignore him. He sat on the floor next to me, at my level. He continued talking as if I wanted to have a conversation. He reached out and bent over my back like he was going to hug me. Then he put his finger into the inviting indentation I was so desperately trying to conceal. I hated him. I was enraged.

I quickly turned around, incensed at his touching me. At that moment I wanted to kill him. I reached into the galvanized bucket of gritty water and clobbered him in the face with the dripping Pine-Sol-soaked sponge. Not once, but over and over again. I screamed "Stop it!" while the water and dirty suds from the kitchen floor ran down his face onto his perfectly pressed Army uniform. At first he looked angry, and then he grinned. That was the last time he ever touched me. He knew to stop. He also knew that I wasn't going to tell. That is why he smiled.

***

A note about the photo at the beginning of this chapter: we had a junk drawer in our kitchen where we had a pile of undeveloped film because we couldn't afford to take them to Walgreens all at the same time. Somehow, this roll languished for years before it ended up in my sister's clutches. I saw it for the first time in a box of pictures we were going through after my 50th birthday.

JUDY FERRARO

This is about the time I started babysitting.

6 MARGARET AND THE BOOGIEMAN

The sexual abuse finally ended after the Pine-Sol incident.
Life moved along. One summer my mother arranged for me
to meet a woman she had met while selling Avon. Her
customer was looking for some responsible and reliable girls
to babysit for her daughter who was just shy of 1 year old.
Once Jeanette and I met Tammy, she called us almost
immediately to take care of Margaret, a beautiful little girl
with blonde hair, blue eyes and the longest eyelashes I had

ever seen. Because of my age, I was given the day jobs while Jeanette made herself available for the evenings.

Tammy and Jack Johnson owned a brick raised ranch in a subdivision built in the 60s called, believe it or not, Jolly Homes. The houses were new and so were the marriages of the young couples who lived there. Their red brick house smelled of newness. The carpet was new; the paint was fresh. The rooms seemed so much larger than the rooms in our home. There was even a room just for watching TV. The separate TV room ensured the living room with its vanilla brocade sectional couch wrapped in plastic, glass tables, and gold-etched mirrored walls remained pristine. There were always good snacks, bottles of soda and sometimes even money to order a pizza. They had a white German shepherd named Prince who made me feel safe. Sometimes Prince barked uncontrollably. I became concerned that someone was trying to get in. Although I was pretty confident if any intruders found their way into the house, Prince would have killed and eaten them. Babysitting at this Jolly Home was like going to paradise and getting paid for the journey.

Jack's family owned a string of drive-in movie theaters and every once in a while, they took me with them. Tammy and Jack were very generous and shared the passes with my family too. They paid us 50 cents an hour and a tip, depending on how long they were gone.

I always cleared my schedule when Tammy called. As I grew older and they got to know me better, they trusted me with evening babysitting. The money was good, the house was great, and the food and snacks were plentiful. There was a phone in practically every room, a teenager's dream. I grew very close to little Margaret. As she became a toddler, I protected her from the Boogieman. Together, we checked her closet and under her bed to make sure her room was Boogieman-free before she went to sleep. Her look of concern melted into a winsome relieved smile. Soon Jack and Tammy added a little brother. Their family was perfect, and I loved it. They were just the way I imagined myself to be when I was old enough to be married.

Then something terrible happened. There was talk of Tammy leaving Jack. She was in love with someone else. She left her perfectly good husband, a beautiful home, great food, a nice family life and unlimited theater tickets.

And then I heard she left all that — for Gil! I was devastated. Her love affair with Gil began at my family's house, the same home where he abused me and wrecked my childhood. Tammy was visiting my mother when he dropped by one day and that snake slithered his way into her life, spewed his venom and ruined it. I never understood Tammy's attraction to Gil, but I didn't address it. I managed to block it all out, just like the sexual abuse. In hindsight, I believe his attraction was to little Margaret.

Margaret was between 4 and 5 when Tammy married Gil, just the age he liked his victims. At that point, my teenage life had begun. I was busy working at the Dairy Castle Diner, first as a carhop in the summer, and then as a short order cook and waitress in the winter. I was on the dance team in high school. I secured a job as a secretary the week I received my diploma. I voted for a United States president, made new friends and played softball for a tavern in Calumet City. I was busy and moving forward. I heard scuttlebutt about Tammy and Gil's marriage but paid little attention. I had lost all respect for Tammy when she left her good life with Jack for a bad one with the monster. Tammy had been kind to me. I should have told her about Gil. I am haunted by regret that I was unable to process my sexual abuse sooner. If I had, perhaps I could have protected little Margaret from the real Boogeyman.

***

Several years later, when I was married and well into my 20s, I received a call from my mother. I was lying on the couch nursing a hangover — that is how I spent Sundays in my 20s. My mother was distraught when she called to share with me the horrible accusations Tammy had made about Gil sexually molesting little Margaret. She had even called the police. My mother was disgusted with Tammy and angry that she would put Gil through such nonsense and ruin his good name. I remember her words, "Have you ever heard anything so crazy?" Memories of my own sexual abuse ran like a tape on fast forward. It was my first time recollecting the abuse. The memories became vivid. I remembered how Gil waited until my parents were gone and the house was dark. He knew I was pretending to be fast asleep. I could feel him slip into bed beside me with the intent to satisfy his sick lust.

I told my mother I was coming over. I wanted to know more about Margaret and Tammy. I wanted to talk to my mother, in person. I put the phone back on the receiver, grabbed my car keys and drove the half hour to my parent's home. My mind was racing — the thoughts, the fear and confusion — all filling my head. If you ask me what route I took, I wouldn't be able to tell you.

My thoughts went from little Margaret to me, then me to Margaret. How long had this been happening to her? Why didn't I step up and tell the beguiled Tammy at the beginning? I could have protected Margaret from the Boogieman! Why didn't I expose him and save Margaret this pain? I didn't think anyone would have listened to me then, but they were going to listen now. As a society, we abhor sexual abuse. But as individuals, we don't want to discuss it. It's easier and nicer to be discreet. It's best to mind our own business. But now I knew that to remain silent was an act of cowardice.

I sat with my mother and shared the stories of the nights she left us alone with Gil. She sat silent, shocked, her face pale and saddened. I couldn't tell if she ever really believed me; there was never any validation. There were no words of acknowledgement, remorse or comfort. She did not say she was sorry about what I had been through. She didn't ask any questions. She just listened. I left with the weight of the world off my shoulders but with guilt in my heart. Why hadn't I shared this sooner? What was wrong with me? I was beginning to process the abuse. But with the processing came anger — at myself.

I doubt my father ever learned of the sexual abuse. I never told him and my mother spent a good part of her life protecting him from any bad news, from the bad behavior and choices of their children to the monthly bills that exceeded the monthly income. I was in a front row seat of the class on keeping secrets and I learned well.

I made calls to Tammy and shared information that I am sure she would have liked to have known many years before. But strangely, she did not leave Gil immediately. I heard they tried counseling. I was disappointed by Tammy and her decision to stay with Gil. Tammy and Gil had another little girl during their marriage who also was abused by Gil. It wasn't until Tammy learned Gil was cheating on her that she finally left him.

I don't really know what happened to Margaret or her sister. My own sister has conversations with Tammy from time to time. I couldn't bring myself to respect Tammy as a person anymore. Gil ruined the lives of everyone she loved. Her good life was over the moment she left her lovely home and moved her children to live with the man who was destined to sexually abuse her daughters.

Several years later, Gil was arrested at a police prostitution sting in a south suburb of Chicago. My mother called to tell me. Finally, the validation I desperately needed from her. His name was read on TV and there was a video of him being arrested. That sick bastard couldn't stop. The list of victims kept growing. Gil spent his teenage years shredding the life of at least one young girl on the block where he lived, then progressed to his step-daughter Margaret, and then his own daughters — the one with Tammy and yet another who resided on the East Coast. Gil was a boy, a teenager and then a man who victimized those who loved, needed and depended on him, and like the plague, he spread his sickness and poison everywhere he went. I wonder how many lives were affected by his behavior. My guess is dozens and that some have never been able to emerge from the deep dark hole he dug for them.

***

After the initial conversation with my mother about Gil abusing Margaret, I went to the library and checked out several books about sexual abuse. I read them all, trying to understand how this could have happened. Why hadn't I told? How do I get through this?

I am convinced that my first marriage was damaged before it ever began. I had not addressed the issues of my molestation. I never told my first husband, not even the night I told my mother I was sexually abused. I just distanced myself and finally left him. I needed help. I wanted to be rescued.

If I had to do it all over again, I would have asked my mother to go to therapy with me. I would have learned to forgive her for not noticing that something was terribly wrong in my childhood. I would have forgiven myself for not speaking up to spare the other victims. I should have reached out to Margaret at the right time. To this day, I think about calling her.

I understand now that when my mother shared further information about Gil and his sexual scandals, it was her way of telling me she believed me. She was not a trained counselor and had never personally experienced sexual abuse. I wish she could have offered me guidance. I could have prepared myself for the future, when I was forced to come face to face with the Boogeyman.

My knight in shining armor, my brother Spike and I during the Blizzard of '67.

7 THE FUNERALS AND THE FONDLER

Life is filled with irony. The very person who was responsible for stealing my innocence was the son of a woman whom I adored. She gave me attention when I needed it. She instilled confidence in me by focusing on my talents throughout my childhood.

Sandy Zampari was Gil's mother. Our relationship began

when I was almost 5. I was walking past her beautifully manicured front lawn, admiring the colorful tulips that surrounded her home. There were hundreds of tulips in every color imaginable. Red, orange, yellow, red with yellow, orange with red. They were beautiful and something that was nonexistent in our yard due to my dad's knack for carelessly decapitating my mother's flowers with the lawnmower.

Because the flowers in our yard never had a chance, I was attracted to the blooming garden on our block. I proceeded to pick a few blossoms, preparing a bouquet for my deserving mother. Mrs. Zampari was friendly with my mom and a nice neighbor lady who surely wouldn't miss a few tulips. After all, she had hundreds of them. I proudly brought the colorful bouquet to my mom. This gesture filled with love would surely bring a smile to my beautiful mother's face. It did. It also brought an inquisition of sorts about where I had happened upon the lovely flowers. I was sent to Mrs. Zampari's house to apologize. When all was said and done, my mother had a vase full of tulips, and I had Mrs. Zampari. She accepted the apology and invited me to help her plant bulbs the following fall. That way, when I picked the flowers for my mother, they were half mine and I was no longer pillaging our neighbor's garden.

Sandy was born and raised on the Delaware shore. She shared so many of her hometown stories with me that I could drift off during our conversations and feel as if I had been there myself. I longed to walk on the sandy beach and stay in a clapboard house. I imagined the waves lapping the shore as families enjoyed picnics in the sand and staying at the beach until the sun set. Sandy gave me the greatest gift anyone can give a person: time. She shared her interests with me. Her art lessons became my art lessons. She played the piano beautifully and allowed me to pound away on the one in her orderly living room. I didn't get much further than chopsticks, but I developed a desire to play the piano and the instinct to know that I belonged in music. I still play a pretty good rendition of "Heart and Soul."

Up to the day she died when I was in my 30s, Sandy and I shared a very special relationship. She listened to me sing, took an interest in my studies, and shared her love of the arts with me. She was my biggest fan. I believe she would have been devastated if she had known what her son did to me.

Our visits were fewer once I got married and went out on my own. Possibly it was that I had recollected the abuse and wanted to distance myself. Yet we wrote cards and letters to stay in touch and always remembered each other's birthday. My mom called to tell me that Sandy's husband had died. I felt anxious when I thought about paying my respects. I didn't want to run into her child-molester son. I hadn't seen him in years. I had gone through sessions with two different therapists in an attempt to overcome the sexual abuse. Neither one had prepared me for a reunion.

I called a couple of family members who knew about the abuse for moral support. I was looking for protection. I wanted to be there for Sandy, but I didn't want to attend the funeral alone. My mother stated that she and my father would be attending early to avoid the crowd. My brother wasn't sure how his day was shaking out and couldn't promise to be there at any specific time. Being unavailable for support is typical behavior of families who have decided to shelve the issue. I put Sandy's feelings before my own and set out for the wake. After all, she had lost her husband. I couldn't depend on my family. I had been through worse, and I could do this.

As I drove to the familiar funeral parlor in my home town, I ran scenario after scenario through my head. What would I say? Who else would be there? Whom would I know? Where should I park? I remember crying to think that my mother and brother did not or could not support me. Was that their form of denial? Why wouldn't they come to terms with the fact that I was abused? I pulled myself together and drove my car into the small L-shaped gravel parking lot that wrapped around the building. As I put the car in park, I could feel my heart pounding.

I approached the back entrance and looked up to see my brother Spike outside the back door amidst all the smokers, waiting for me. I felt so relieved, supported and empowered. I could walk into the wake with my head held high, my brother at my side, just in case. I don't really know what could have happened. Scratching out the eyes of the widow's grown son would have surely made the local papers. I spotted Gil immediately. His face was puffy and his clothes, like his face, looked worn. His good looks were gone.

As we walked to the casket, he extended his hand as if we were old business acquaintances. I looked him square in the eye and said, "Too bad it isn't you lying in the casket." He gave me an "Oh come on…." sort of look and I moved on, leaving him behind, knowing that I had finally awakened from that "pretend" sleep of mine. I made it clear that I loathed him, and he stayed as far away from me as possible. His body language changed and his swagger waned. It took nearly 30 years, but the balance of power had shifted!

At the wake, I was able to spend some time with Sandy and told her how sorry I was about the death of her husband. But I really wasn't. He was a crabby old Italian guy who chain smoked cigarettes and drank beer in the driveway when he wasn't at the neighborhood tavern boozing himself into oblivion. His language was crude and I'm not sure if I ever saw him smile. I sometimes wondered if he was the source of Gil's problems. I continued to correspond with Sandy after her husband died and visited her when I was in the neighborhood. But a few years later, she, too, passed away.

***

Once again, when Sandy died, I was faced with another funeral home visit and an encounter with the child molester. I walked past him as though he were invisible. There was no need for concern; he didn't dare come anywhere close to where I stood. He was afraid of me. He was now a coward.

A relative of Sandy's asked me to visit her home and choose some artwork that she had stored in a box in her closet. Her generosity meant so much to me. The thought of Sandy wanting me to have something to remember her by was touching. At that particular moment, I was so glad that Sandy never found out about her son's sickness.

I chose two of Sandy's creations. They are lovely pieces of art: one is a modern watercolor, the other an intricate pen and ink. I was a little worried where they might take me when I looked at them, but Gil never entered my mind when I chose them, framed them, or hung them on the walls of our home. I love Sandy's artwork. They help me remember our art lessons when she taught me how to shade objects and the importance of painting with different-sized brushes. I'm glad I had her in my life. Although she bore a monster, she was inspirational. We shared a special relationship that began with stolen tulips.

***

A few years later, I heard that Gil had died. I don't know how he died and I don't care. I just knew that I would be better off when he was dead and so would he. My sister called to tell me. I think she may have attended the wake. I'm not sure if anyone in my family ever believed my story — or should I say — wanted to believe my story. The good news is that he was gone and the bad news is that I am not the only woman who was glad to see him go. Unfortunately, people like Gil are so toxic that long after they are dead and gone, those affected have pain and confusion that festers and reemerges. Sometimes at a gas station.

JUDY FERRARO

Great friends Barb and Jim accompanied me to court.

8 TAKING CHASE

This fall day in 1985 started like any other day, with the alarm sounding at 6:30 a.m. My hand reflexively hit the snooze button and I turned over to catch a few more moments of sleep. The autumn sky was grey and light rain dampened the windows. Even my hungry cat didn't budge. It was a good day to sleep in, call in sick, and play hooky. But this day in my 30th year would be different. I could never have guessed how significant it would become in my life.

Twenty minutes later, after a few rounds of the snooze-button exercise and the relentless sound of my alarm, I was readying myself for a day on the road. I was in sales and had several customers to visit that particular day. I was driving a loaner while my own car was in my brother Spike's shop. I had scheduled the day efficiently. I would be visiting existing accounts and dropping off sales literature for a few potential clients. The plan was to get my car at the end of the day and maybe get in a home-cooked meal with my parents. I showered, brushed my teeth, put on some makeup and a pair of black pants with a jacket to match, fed my cat, and was on my way.

While driving from my apartment on the north side of Chicago to visit my customers in the south suburbs, I felt the wheel of the loaner pulling to the right, but didn't think much of it. After all, in a few short hours I would be dropping off this clunker for my own repaired vehicle. After my second customer visit, I felt the car drifting far to the right, even with my hands using more force to keep it under control. Luckily, there was a gas station just ahead. I pulled into the station close to the pay phone. Cell phones were mounted in cars back then, but the loaner did not provide me that luxury. I would call Spike from the pay phone and ask him to change my tire. I looked in the trunk. No spare. Great, the rest of my day was shot. I had things to do, customers to see. I should have stayed in bed with the cat.

There was a tall African-American man standing at the service island using the pay phone. I anxiously fumbled through the bottom of my purse for some change to make my call. When I looked up to see if he had completed his call, I was faced with the unthinkable. He had his penis in his hand, masturbating. Fear of rape was my immediate reaction. I quickly used my elbow to lock the car door. In retrospect, I probably should have leaned on the horn or started the ignition to drive the hobbling car away, but in that moment of panic, those practical actions never crossed my mind. Who in the world is prepared for that situation?

I looked away, not knowing what to do. Using my peripheral vision, I looked again. And at that moment he spewed semen all over the loaner car window. I couldn't believe my eyes. He then took a yellow tissue out of his right pocket and wiped himself clean. Calmly, he pulled himself together, zipped his pants and began to walk away. Rage overtook my fear. I was incensed. Without thought, I opened the loaner car door, got out, and took chase. He turned his head, surprised to see my aggressive reaction, and his swaggering walk turned into a sprint. Gil flashed through my mind. I yelled, "If I catch you, I will kill you!" I meant it, and he knew it.

He ran while repeatedly looking back over his shoulder.

He dashed through a field and into a cul-de-sac where his maroon Monte Carlo was parked. He frantically got in and drove away, leaving me just yards behind him. I memorized his license plate number and ran back to the gas station to call the police. To this day, I'm not sure what I would have done if I had caught him. And I could see by the look on his face that he didn't care to find out.

The gas station attendants were helpful but I could tell they were amused as well. I called the police from their business phone and then I called my brother. The police arrived and were pleased that I had gotten the license plate number which would make their job a little easier. Spike was dumbfounded. He couldn't believe that I chased the guy. What if he had a gun or a knife? That's the question asked every time I share this story. And I don't have an answer. Perhaps my weapon of blind fury fueled with adrenalin caused by my terrible childhood memories would have protected me. And as disgusting and potentially dangerous as that situation was, it resulted in a catharsis for me and my long-held child abuse horrors. I wasn't going to let any man get away with that. Not now.

After filling out the proper paperwork, the police asked Spike and me to ride with them to the house of the suspect. Two police cars drove to the house. My brother and I were in the back seat of the unmarked squad car and parked across the street. The other one pulled into the driveway behind the Monte Carlo, license plate number 8524974. The man who accosted me answered the door in a white terry cloth robe. Apparently he went home and showered after our chase. He didn't want any evidence, I thought. What an idiot! The evidence was right there on the loaner car window. The police asked me if that was the man I had seen at the gas station. Of course it was. Spike kept muttering that he didn't like the way the police were handling the situation. Since he now knew where the offender lived, I believe he wanted to handle it himself. I appreciated that he wanted to beat the guy bloody, but I wanted to use the system to get this sick bastard. It was what I should have done with Gil. It was, in a way, a second chance.

The police asked the robed man, whose name was Darrell, to dress and go to the police station where there was paperwork and a charge of indecent exposure. After a few trips to court and continuance after continuance, the charges were dropped. Darrell had hired a slick lawyer who wore a navy pin-striped, three-piece suit complete with a red carnation in the lapel. He found a way to beat the system for his client; the charges were dropped because the police had failed to present him in a line-up. They also failed to take a sample of his semen from the car window. The system had let me down. I could have prevailed by hiring my own attorney.

But, once again, I chose silence.

After the continuances and Darrell's acquittal came the fear that this pervert was angry and would find me because I pressed charges. I removed my phone number from directory assistance and the phone book to make myself more difficult to find. I tried to put it all behind me despite the frequent requests from friends to retell the story. They were amused and telling the story seemed to empower me.

Fast forward three years. An assistant state's attorney whom I had dated a few times called me. "Guess whose name came up at lunch today?" he asked. "I wouldn't know," I replied. "Yours. And some pervert's you chased through a field a few years ago. Do you remember him?"

My first thought was that my friend had somehow found out that Darrell was coming after me. I was wrong. It seems Darrell was caught masturbating outside a girl's dormitory in Georgia and exposing himself to the coeds. More victims, I thought, remorsefully. I should have prevailed when the charges were dropped against him. "Once a sex offender, always a sex offender," my friend would tell me.

Once again, my decision to keep silent had created more victims.

While Darrell was not convicted of my charges at the gas station on that cold, rainy fall morning, the story could be used to convict him of his latest crimes. It seems there was a long list of incidents, but no convictions. My assistant state's attorney friend forewarned me that I would be receiving a subpoena. I told him I was not going to court anymore and waste time on this derelict from my past. "Time has passed and I have put that incident behind me," I told him. He politely replied that subpoenas didn't work that way and that he would see me at my deposition. Great, I thought.

I was subpoenaed and interviewed by two young prosecutors who were very, very eager to get a conviction. They were confident that my testimony would win their case and Darrell would soon be behind bars. Next step: a jury trial where I would be the witness. More wasted time, I thought.

The night before my early morning court date, I had dinner with the niece and nephew of a dear friend. Barbara and Jim were moving to Chicago and I was asked to show them around. It was a nice evening with these new friends — interesting conversation, cocktails and good food. Unfortunately, I explained, I couldn't stay out late because I had to show up for an early court date the next morning. My new friend Barbara was, quite coincidentally, a student of criminology and was very interested. I had the opportunity, once again, to amuse fresh ears with my "pervert" story. Concerned, they offered to join me the next day in court. It had never crossed my mind to ask anyone to accompany me. I truly thought that there would be another continuance, or perhaps the case would be thrown out of court yet again.

The next morning Barbara and Jim met me at the courthouse bright and early. Barbara was correct in her assumption; there would be a trial that day. I was a witness and only allowed in the courtroom during my own testimony. My new friends, however, were able to travel in and out and keep me apprised of what was happening.

While I was testifying, Darrell's lawyer — the same slick one in the same three-piece navy pin-striped suit with an identical red carnation in his lapel — began to question me:

"Where are you from?"

"Midlothian."

"Where do you live now?"

"Chicago."

"How many black people do you know?"

"Lots, maybe hundreds."

"How much do you think I weigh?"

"Two hundred pounds."

"How tall do you think I am?"

"6'2"."

I didn't know where he was going with this questioning. Darrell's lawyer declared that my identification of the suspect was incorrect. Because I incorrectly guessed his weight and height, he took the desperate approach that all black people looked the same to me.

I was furious. Instinct kicked in and I wanted to chase him, too, only this time from my chair in the witness box.

"What about my client makes him different from any other black man you've seen in your life?" he asked. "The truth is, Judy, that all black men look the same to you. What makes this man different from any other black man?"

And the chase ensued. I deliberately and angrily began, "The reason that that black man," I pointed my finger at Darrell, "is different is because he is the only black man who stood beside me at a gas station, practically masturbated in my face, ejaculated on my car window, took a yellow tissue out of his pocket, cleaned his penis, zipped up his pants and then ran to his maroon Monte Carlo parked in a cul-de-sac just behind a gas station, license plate number 8524974, drove to his house where he parked the same car in the driveway and later opened the door wearing a white terry cloth robe." The details came back to me with remarkable clarity — as if it had all happened yesterday. I concluded emphatically, "That's what makes him different from any other black man I have known in my life. No other black man has ever done that to me."

The young female prosecutor threw her pencil into the air, her smile larger than her face. She and her partner did everything but a high five and a chest bump. My new friends Jim and Barbara sat on their hands to keep from clapping. I was ushered out of the courtroom where more testimony was heard. My friends and I went to my apartment and several hours later received a call that Darrell had been convicted. He would spend the next 11 months in prison.

Later, in a therapy session, I learned that this may have been the event that allowed me to turn a sharp corner in my healing process. I hadn't told on Gil. I didn't protect myself from him. But I did go after this man who violated me. I chased him. I prosecuted him. He was found not guilty the first time, and then I was called again. This time I got him.

Anyone who knows me understands that I have enough sense to lean on the horn or drive off in such a situation. But that day, something clicked. I was angry and I followed that anger. I was being violated and I wasn't going to let that happen again. I protected myself. Something changed on that rainy fall day. Courage overcame fear. That courage was extremely important because I was about to make some vital decisions in my life. The most vital of those decisions was to start therapy.

By the time I was in 8ᵗʰ grade, I had completely blocked out that I was abused.

9 BRAIN REPAIR & MAINTENANCE

"Who were you chasing through the field that day, Darrell or Gil?" Dr. Pearlstein, one of my professional therapists would eventually ask.

***

My initial "do-it-yourself" therapy started shortly after I heard about Gil's sexual encounters with little Margaret. After reading several books, I felt healed. My life was under control. For the time being, I had it beat; the demons were gone. I had come to the conclusion that I was better off because there was never actual penetration. Hopelessly, I clung to that fact. I told myself I was lucky that my abuse was less serious than that of others. And so I delayed getting the right type of help.

It is unfortunate that I let so much time pass before seeking professional therapy. Trying to work things out independently was just another way of keeping my dreadful secret to myself. During the years when most 20-year-olds were going to college and creating a career path, I was making my way up a mudslide. Everything fast and furious without progress. I like to call those my "wonder years" because I wonder what happened. So many drunken nights, bad dates and weak relationships. The result of the recklessness was a dive in self-esteem and a lot of close calls.

Many unhealthy behaviors more dangerous than mine are the result of childhood abuse. It causes a smorgasbord of dysfunction: amnesia, anorexia, obesity, promiscuity, sexual dysfunction, depression and suicide, to name a few. Low self-esteem can lead to relationship issues, alcoholism, drug addiction and multiple marriages. Sexual abuse survivors long for intimacy but when intimacy is found, we don't know how to handle ourselves in the relationship. We move on. We run.

Once in therapy, I found that talking to a professional whose job is to steer you in the right direction is great — at times gratifying but sometimes painful. I believe everyone should have therapy with the same frequency they get the oil changed on their cars. There should be little stickers on our windshields or blinking alarms on our dashboards reminding us after so many miles of life to get a therapy checkup. The average person spends heaps of time and hard-earned money keeping automobiles, wardrobes and physical appearances maintained. We pay hundreds of dollars a year for cable and cell phones. But some of the same people find it difficult to spend their dollars on emotional maintenance. If only hair stylists were required to have PhDs in psychology, we would be allowed to multitask while getting coiffed. They could work on both the inside and outside of our heads. The salon could be called "Heal or Dye". But I doubt Heal or Dye would stay in business for long because those in denial would never return.

I once attended a seminar where the speaker asked the audience how many people had relatives with heart disease. Dozens of hands flew into the air. Second question: how many people have relatives with diabetes? Even more hands flew into the air. The third question: how many people have relatives with mental illness or could use therapy for an event that has occurred in their lifetime? It was as if the entire room was sitting on their hands until a couple of stragglers sheepishly raised their hands. No one wants to admit they, or anyone they know, are in the process of obtaining or needing therapy — brain repair and maintenance, as I like to call it.

Even though I desired help, I couldn't bring myself to take the necessary steps to actually get the help I so desperately needed. Perhaps I didn't know how. It was in my early 30s when I realized I needed a professional. I was having dinner with a friend who shared that she had been sexually abused by an uncle and was undergoing therapy 25 years later. Her story helped me realize that I needed therapy, too. Her ordeal seemed worse than mine, because her abuser was a relative. I continued to cling to the fact that my abuse was less damaging, as if it were a saving grace. I asked her for the name of her therapist and made an appointment.

When I went to see my first therapist, she asked me to call her by her first name, Maria. As I poured out my deepest, darkest secrets, she actually stood up to go look at herself in one of the many mirrors hanging on the wall of her office. I wondered if she liked what she saw in her reflection.

She began by asking me an endless list of questions and made notes on a yellow legal pad. As I spoke, she kept writing furiously. I wondered if she was scribbling notes about what I was communicating to her or what she thought about what I was communicating to her. No one had ever taken such an interest in me. Each answer would provoke another question. She asked repeatedly, "…and how did that make you feel?" I liked that she wanted to know how I felt. I walked through life feeling bad, betrayed, used and invisible. I hoped Maria could help me end the negative and bring on the positive.

She asked about my relationships, all of them: family, friends, relatives, and, of course, my romantic relationship history. I was able to give her an earful about my ex-boyfriend who slapped me around when I didn't iron his pants. I was glad to get that off my chest; I should have gone for therapy immediately after that dreadful moment. Surely, I endured his behavior the same way I had learned early on how to deal with bad behaviors — by believing somehow that they were my fault and then blocking them out.

I stay in friendships with people who are substance abusers. I do not enable them. Their abuse is inflicted upon themselves, by themselves. But I stick around, perhaps because I was programmed to tolerate the dysfunction, or maybe because I don't want to leave them. I know what it feels like to desperately need help without seeking professional assistance. Like the Bible verses I like so much, it is their "time to break down," I want to be beside them when it's their "time to build up."

The more I shared with Maria, the more I began to see

the patterns in my life. I was able to visualize a timeline of my life but certain segments were missing. Poof! If I didn't think about them, they were just gone. I thought they had been erased. That was my coping mechanism. Erasure.

When I started to tell Maria about the pedophile who was asked to babysit for my siblings and me, she began writing faster and faster. From where I sat, it looked like chicken scratch. I hoped there were answers in her detailed notes about my life.

In future visits, however, the conversations became more and more painful. Maria's questions forced me to divulge my well-kept secret not only to her, but also to myself. Talking about it made it seem real again, just like writing this book does. Fifty minutes was not enough time. I often left Maria's office in tears. Between visits, I made notes and wrote questions to ask her. I began to understand my life path. My choices were clarified.

Fortunately, I was able to tell her my traumatic story. Many survivors cannot. Revealing the awful secret is more than some can manage. When this is the case, group therapy is often the answer. In a setting of empathetic individuals who have been similarly violated, it seems less difficult. I knew group therapy would send me into a spin with each new story, so I avoided it. This issue of secrecy is often the behavior that prevents us from developing true relationships with family, friends, coworkers and romantic partners. In the telling of my alarming story, I was able to find humor. Maria liked that about me. I'm so grateful for my sense of humor. I have depended on it my whole life. So much was stolen, but Gil wasn't able to take that from me.

My therapy brought on anger. Anger at myself for not sharing my experience with my parents and anger at Gil for the pedophilia. Surely my parents would have listened to me, and my father, uncles, and cousins would have wrung the neck of the freckle-faced teenager who molested me. I began to wonder if my life would have been different had I told. There was an endless list of "what ifs."

The therapy produced feelings of contempt for Gil. It brought me to suffer embarrassment about some of my behaviors from grade school on into adulthood. I was filled with grief and a longing for the way life could have been. I had a desire for revenge. But even then, I didn't go to the police. My mother told me that too much time had passed and I believed her. I also felt the need to protect Gil's mother, my dear neighbor-lady friend, Sandy, from the pain. And besides, as I continuously told myself, there was no penetration; I was lucky. I already falsely convinced myself of that.

After getting the facts, Maria recommended that she hypnotize me in order to relive the sexual abuse. I wasn't sure

I wanted to go back to that place in time. The thought of enduring those awful moments frightened me. How could I live through it again?

***

I had been easily hypnotized once before by an entertainer named John Lautrec. I was in my early 20s, and he was featured at a club in our area. He hypnotized me by softly repeating phrases like "Your arms are heavy, you're relaxed. Your head is heavy." Once hypnotized, he sent me on a journey into the audience to give the "best-looking guy" a kiss. My friends told me I walked around for 10 minutes as guys yelled out, "Pick me, pick me!" but apparently I couldn't decide. As the audience howled with laughter, I walked back and forth among several men, finally chose one who was on a date with another woman, and kissed him. I don't remember a thing. My friends still remind me of that evening — all that entertainment for a mere $5 cover charge.

So I knew I was a good candidate for hypnotherapy. During the hypnosis, Maria asked me to use my adult brain in the body of my 5-year-old self. The session was recorded by either video or audio, I don't remember. What I do remember is the discussion about my response to Maria's questions. She walked me through an episode as I had described to her in the prior sessions.

"Your mother is asking Gil to watch her children. What

happens?" I am cringing because I don't like that Gil takes care of us. Will he come into my room or leave me alone? What I will do if he comes in the room? But everyone else seemed happy that Gil was taking care of us.

I knew I would do what I always did; I would pretend that I was sleeping. If I were sleeping, I could act as if the abuse didn't happen or I didn't know it happened. And the next day could be normal.

"Gil is entering your room, he lies in the bed behind you, and you feel his warm breath on the back of your neck. His hand starts to rub your back. What should you do?" And just like Maria thought would happen, my life experience and matured brain reacted. There would be no sexual abuse. I would call out to my siblings as he touched me. I would bite him until he bled and scratch at his eyes. My fists would hit him and the screaming wouldn't stop until the neighbors heard me. I would ask my mother to find a different babysitter and never let Gil into our home again. I would call the police. I would tell everyone — my parents, grandmother, uncles and cousins — what he did. And there would be no waiting. If I told them immediately, they would protect me from the monster. Together with my parents we would call the authorities and Gil would immediately be prosecuted. He would be behind bars and unable to harm other young girls. Maybe he would get the help he really needed and have a better life for himself. My family comforted me while I was hypnotized. They would never let anything happen to me again.

Maria's guidance allowed me to look into a mirror of my own, relive the horrible past through the eyes of a strong and powerful adult, and move towards healing. I looked in the mirror and liked what I saw.

I learned that none of the abuse was my fault. I didn't have the emotional intelligence to protect myself. I was never warned about sexual abuse or given the protocol on what to do if I were touched inappropriately. Even now, not every child is given those tools.

I'm not sure hypnosis cured me, but it got me from a bad place into a better place. I read even more about sexual abuse and the books began to make sense to me. I was no longer the victim of sexual abuse. I was now a warrior in a quest to heal myself from the effects of sexual abuse. I wrapped up my sessions with Maria and moved on with my life.

***

Five years after I was hypnotized by Maria, I started seeing another therapist. A man I was dating asked me to go to counseling with him. He had been married twice before and was falling in love with me and me with him. He didn't want to duplicate past relationship mistakes and thought therapy was the answer. I reluctantly agreed to accompany him to a few sessions; I gave him the benefit of the doubt. After all, he was quite handsome and I liked that he was willing to work on our relationship in its infancy. This handsome man eventually became my second husband. After a couple of joint sessions and a mention of my sexual abuse, the counselor asked to see me separately. I suspected that would happen.

Dr. Pearlstein was a wonderful young woman from the Middle East. She had a strong accent and was difficult for me to understand her at times. Nevertheless, her therapy significantly affected our lives as individuals and as a couple. First and foremost, she taught us the importance of working on our relationship. We learned to fight fairly, and most important, respectfully. While we are formed by our own families, we can follow those familiar and possibly dysfunctional behavior patterns or make a new mold, which is what we decided to do.

Dr. Pearlstein was able to find all the positive strides in my development and recovery. She focused on my strengths and how I had beaten the odds. We discussed how there really weren't any signs of sexual abuse for my parents to see. Although I masturbated excessively as a child (even once in a room with my grandmother) and engaged in sexual play with friends using Barbie and Ken as the example, my mother never found out. I sucked my thumb until I was 11, about the time when the abuse ended. But just like the abuse, I concealed my behaviors.

Dr. Pearlstein assured me that many young children explore their sexuality in a variety of ways. She also felt strongly that I wasn't the only one in the house being abused by Gil. I was asked to stop thinking that it could have been worse. Penetration was not the determining factor of whether it was bad or very bad. It was all bad.

I also was reminded that my strong male relationships developed regardless of my molestation experiences. My father, brother, uncles and male cousins and friends are some of the strongest relationships in my life, past and present. My long-term, serious relationships were the right choices.

After three visits, I started to forgive my mother and myself. I learned about family dynamics. I learned how to manage my resentment. I learned that I had good parents who loved me, and I loved them. Like most parents, they did their best with the tools they were given. Before this second round of therapy, I had lumped together any and all of my "emotional issues" as a result of being sexually abused as a child. I learned that some of my dysfunctional behaviors and pain were related to other experiences. Other behaviors were just normal. It was nice to feel normal, a way I had seldom thought of myself.

I remember crying during sessions with Dr. Pearlstein.

Learning about oneself and accepting life as it is dished out is difficult. If I had never accepted the abuse and moved beyond it, I might still be jumping in and out of relationships, looking to be saved by someone, anyone.

Writing this book has been therapeutic — but difficult at times. I know I am not finished with therapy. It is time for another round of brain "repair and maintenance." I am glad I continue my relationship with therapy. I visit another therapist sporadically now and it is a comfort knowing that there is a professional on hand to guide me. I have spoken very little about the sexual abuse with my current therapist, Dr. Sobel. The experience no longer controls me, although she asks questions about my feelings, reminding me that I am not completely healed.

Therapy has taught me how to recover when I am falling backward. It helped me understand and appreciate the roles people played in my life and healing process. Therapy is where I learned there was much more good than bad.

JUDY FERRARO

Dad and his brothers from left:
Dad and Uncles Gabe, Jerry and Bernie

Cousin Gary and I with Toni
and Mark in Cheyenne.

My mother's brother,
Uncle Bill

My cousins, from left: Charlie, Billy,
Wes and Brian

10 THE GOOD GUYS

I found through therapy that one of the reasons I survived
was the strong relationships I developed and shared with my
father, brother, uncles and male cousins. Being sexually
abused at such an early age prompted me to believe that every
male was destined to betray or hurt me. That was not the
case.

I have not shared my story with many men, but I have

been able to tell my Uncle Bernie. When I was a child, he was the stereotypical Italian bachelor who lived at home with his parents until well into his 30s. In my grandparents' very meticulous home on Chicago's South Side, Uncle Bernie's room had two single beds. The extra bed was for any of the grandchildren who stayed overnight. Bernie was always out carousing at the time I went to bed. In the wee hours of the morning, I could hear him enter the room. I lay awake worrying that he might climb into bed with me as Gil had. No matter how many times I stayed in that room, I never stopped fearing that he would slide in next to me on my bed. Gil made me suspicious of all men. Adding to that perception was my discovery of Uncle Bernie's Playboy magazines under his bed. I remember thinking he must have "dirty" thoughts and surely he would approach me. He never did.

My Uncle Bernie took me to Chicago for White Sox games, food joints only locals would know about, and Old Town and Rush Street to people watch. He bought my older sister and me paper dresses from a head shop that carried hippie paraphernalia such as incense and bongs. Because of Uncle Bernie, I listened to great music — Louie Prima, Frank Sinatra, Tony Bennett. Everything I enjoyed with him as a kid, I appreciate even more as an adult.

My dad had two more brothers, Gabe and Jerry, with whom I shared close relationships. Uncle Jerry was my godfather. He was witty and warmhearted. Uncle Gabe became my dancing partner at family events. On my mother's side, her brother Bill generously paid me an allowance when I stayed at his house for a week every summer. He made me feel like I belonged. His four sons were my closest cousins while growing up. We slept in a large dorm-like room or on the screened-in front porch on hot summer nights. I was never afraid that they would touch me. I trusted them. None of these wonderful men ever violated me. I remember wondering, "Could this be the way it is supposed to be? Could I be safe with any or all of them?"

One evening when I was 19, I attended a rock concert in Denver with my long-haired, hippie cousin Gary. On our long drive back to our aunt and uncle's home in Cheyenne, Wyoming, he pulled the car to the side of a very dark rural highway. He ordered me to get out. I was frightened of snakes, wild animals and his goofy behavior. He then ordered me to close my eyes and lie on the hood of the car, face up. I was terrified. Then he told me to open my eyes and yelled, "Did you ever see so many freaking stars?" (That's not exactly what he said.) Tension drained out of me and I laughed, replying that no, I had never seen so many freaking stars. And once again, I got the message that all men were not like Gil. In fact, Gil was the terrible exception in male behavior. Each such episode with the good men in my life reinforced my belief that men could be pretty nice people, after all. Time and experience strengthened this faith.

As long as I can remember, my father was my favorite person in the whole world. He was also my brother Spike's favorite person, so I had to share him. The two of us spent time alone with our dad on the family boat. Dad a Navy veteran, claimed to know all things about the ships docked in the Chicago River and crossing Lake Michigan. He told us where they were from, where they might be going, and why. Spike and I learned to recognize the flags of other countries, the kinds of cargo being shipped, and the importance of tug boats. How I cherish those days with my father and my brother.

But then there were my teenage romantic relationships. They were never easy and often fraught with drama. Even though I trusted my relatives, I wasn't so sure about other males. Sexually driven adolescent boys frightened the crap out of me.

During my junior year of high school, I heard about an upperclassman who was interested in me. (Just for the record, by now I had lost the glittery glasses and never replaced them, opting for eye strain.) Brad, this gentle giant, became my high school boyfriend and he made me feel good about myself. He came from a nice family, drove a yellow GTO convertible, and I felt cool and popular when I was with him. His parents included me when they went out to dinner and invited me to family parties. His father was kind and his mother got me a job at her office.

Brad was a nice boy who loved me. My dad nicknamed him "Kong" because he was so big and tall. He converted to Catholicism and gave me a pre-engagement ring while I was still in high school. Being in love with him was confusing. Like most teenagers, we didn't know the difference between love and lust. What was right? What was wrong? Was it all right for someone who said he loves me to fondle me? What was love, exactly? I had already had orgasms and wanted more. That was all right, wasn't it? But boys that age were looking for orgasms, too, and I'd heard that was wrong. I was in conflict.

Brad and I broke up shortly after I graduated from high school. I was too young to be engaged. Although Brad would have done anything for me, I didn't know how to receive that kind of love. His parents were disappointed in me.

My next serious relationship was three years later with my first husband. I married him because I didn't think anyone else would ask me. I had absolutely zero self-esteem. Luckily for me, he was another kind and gentle man. He complimented me on the very things I didn't like about myself. Bill shoveled the path to my car before there were snow blowers. He combed my long black hair to relax me. I loved his family, especially his mother, who influenced me in many positive ways. But when Bill snuggled up beside me, thoughts of Gil crashed through my mind and I pushed him away.

I wanted to be a good wife. He spent as much time at work as he could because that's what he thought was right for our marriage. In reality, we needed more time together because I felt lonely without him. Without his companionship and the counseling I desperately needed, the marriage didn't have a chance. I left him. It wasn't his fault. Years later I called him to apologize but he was still hurt and angry. I understand. He didn't deserve what I did to him. His parents were also disappointed in me.

***

With my second marriage to Mike, my journey of shame ended and a new, healthier one began. He is the one person responsible for taking me to my much-needed therapy and has been my partner for more than two decades. He is kind and gentle. Together we are on the same path. We work side by side raising our son, entertaining in our home and traveling. We are comfortable and content, even in silence. We can always depend on each other. Our relationship is successful because I have been open and truthful with him about my sexual abuse. I communicate my thoughts and fears, and while he respects them, I can tell that it is uncomfortable conversation for him.

I know that the men who had relationships with me before my therapy must have been confused by my behavior. I found it difficult to trust or rely on them. I feel bad when I think of how I must have made them feel. Because I hadn't addressed the abuse, the odds of my having a long-term, successful relationship with any man were slim to none. I hope that they can forgive me someday.

I have come to realize that having relationships with kind and gentle men became a pattern for me — a very good pattern which probably saved me from further trauma and abuse. Not all survivors are so fortunate. So many devastating and unhealthy behaviors — more dangerous than mine — are the result of childhood abuse.

I am eternally grateful for my husband's encouragement to attend therapy. It has helped me daily to move forward. It is the path to a happy, healthy and loving relationship. For many of us therapy is essential for healing. And after all, healing is the desired goal.

JUDY FERRARO

Here I am at the time of my combo Communion and Confirmation — the Molly Shannon character Mary Katherine Gallagher look-alike.

11 THE CATHOLIC CHURCH

I feel the need to explain how the Catholic Church continues to open the wounds of my childhood. With each new pedophilia story, my heart aches for the victims, and my resentment of the church hierarchy increases.

During my youth, Sunday morning trips to church were

not a priority for my family: my dad left the house in the wee hours of the morning to go fishing and my mother didn't drive. The church was a couple of miles away. No wheels, no church. Unlike many of my friends, Sunday mass was never a requirement at our home.

Regardless, some of my favorite childhood memories are of church. My grandmother took me to hers when I visited. It was only a few blocks away and I could hear the church bells from her front porch. I liked the community of that church. My grandparents were always working to help other people. I listened as she sang the hymns that I would someday sing with my own choir. My grandmother almost always wore a hat to church or sometimes she wore what looked like a black, lacy doily on her head. It was a rule back then for women to cover their heads.

I went to church regularly with my friend Joanie when I was 8. She was Methodist and I liked the Sunday school at her church. We drew pictures and sang songs about Jesus. After a couple of years as a Methodist, I remember asking my mother if I was a Catholic. She told me that I was. I then inquired why I didn't go to a Catholic church. Before I knew it, I was enrolled in the dreaded Saturday morning catechism classes taught by nuns dressed in habits who seemed to enjoy their — what seemed to me — hapless lives. Worst of all, it cut into my Saturday morning cartoon time. Instead of watching "Heckle and Jeckle," I was walking a couple of miles, my younger brother in tow, to the Catholic church, rain or shine, to get educated about being a Catholic. Catechism is where Catholics learn about guilt, shame and how to dodge a ruler. Little did they know that I was already very aware of both of those emotions and dodging a ruler headed for my face was a natural reflex. At catechism, I missed the nurturing Sunday school teachers at the Methodist church.

For those of you who are not Catholic, catechism classes are for the non-parochial school students. Those attending the Catholic school receive religion classes in their curriculum. Religion classes are a requirement for all Catholic children to prepare them for their Sacraments of Holy Communion, Confirmation, Confession, Marriage, Holy Orders and Last Rites. Catechism wasn't much fun, but my mother was kind enough to give me some pocket change for candy on the walk home.

Because I started catechism later than most public school kids, I was not on the fast track to Catholicism. The religion classes came with a fee and my parents couldn't afford the expense so our Catholic Sacraments were put on hold. Eventually, I made my first communion in sixth grade, the Sunday before I made my confirmation. I wore a pink pleated mini-dress and a matching pink plastic headband, nothing special. I don't even recall if anyone attended to witness the occasion and I'm certain there's not a photo to remind me of the day. If a big deal had been made, it would be a lasting and significant memory. I do remember a family party where I raked in some cash. I was now a real Catholic, with $49 in the bank and responsibility to my God and my church.

Our parish was St. Christopher's. The church was newly built, suburban and modern. It was spacious and the choir was superb. On Friday nights, St. Chris brought together the children in the community by opening its basement for roller skating. It was the highlight of my week.

Our church had an annual carnival called "The Fiesta." It was a wonderful time for the community. We sold tickets, served Dollar Dinners on Sunday for tips and, of course, rode the hazardous carnival rides that were run by toothless, creepy characters with bad hygiene. It was my favorite time of the summer.

I never wavered. I was happy to attend church in my teens. My family didn't go, so I went with my friends. It was spiritual and social for me. I had lots of fun in church. I used to put Blackjack licorice gum on my front tooth and smile at little kids in front of me when they turned around. I sang at the parish Hootenanny, where Father Gale played his guitar while the children of the parish sang along. I loved being a Catholic and was devoted to my church.

My 20s weren't any different. Even after drinking until all

hours of the morning, I would find a mass that worked into my partying schedule and made sure I attended. When I was married to my first husband who worked most every weekend, I went to church on my own. Even when my friends started to break away from the church, I continued to go. I loved being there.

I remember one Easter in particular. My then-husband was working and I went back to my childhood church, St. Christopher's, for Easter mass. I asked my family to go and fully expected them to be ready and waiting when I arrived to pick them up. They were uninterested and all caught up in the Easter bunny thing. I went to church irritated by the bunny ritual as it has nothing to do with the true meaning of Easter. So off I went, alone. No husband, no family, beaten by the bunny.

I dreaded the part in mass where we were asked to hold hands and recite the Lord's Prayer. I was feeling sorry for myself, alone again, abandoned on Easter. I made up my mind to ignore anyone who wanted to hold hands. I would look away. But the woman next to me was relentless. Her hand reached out for mine. I watched as her hand tried to coax my hand into hers as I resisted. But then she boldly just took it. I was stunned by how much her gesture moved me. Suddenly — in the greatest sense — I wasn't alone. I cried for the rest of the mass. The Lord's Prayer still brings a tear to my eye, every time. I wish I could thank her. Now every chance I have, I reach out and take the hand of the person next to me, just the way my Easter angel did for me. It is interesting how a stranger can change your life that way. I don't remember what she looked like or if she noticed I was crying. I'm just glad she was there. She taught me that I am never really alone. Hers was the hand of God.

Church had been my safe and divine place: happy memories, kind people, and life altering moments. But in my late 20s and early 30s, something sinister happened. The accusations of sexual abuse within the Catholic Church began coming to light. At first, I tried to block them out, much like I had blocked out my own sexual abuse. It felt like a blow from a cannon firing at my head and at my heart. Suddenly my sacred, safe place wasn't safe at all! It was a place where children were abused by those they trusted, just like I was.

Now, decades later, the accusations and convictions continue. Some accusations are linked to the past, others are brand new. Those victims, like me, blocked out their terrible experiences. And suddenly one day, they remembered, just as I had, or finally gained the courage to come forward.

It seemed that Catholic Church sexual abuse allegations were reported weekly. There was no level of the hierarchy that wasn't guilty of either abuse or covering up the abuse. I don't know which betrayal is worse: the pedophiles are sick sinners and those who ignore or hide sexual abuse are criminal liars. The thought of going to confession seemed ridiculous and hypocritical. Confessing my sins to a pedophile or someone who would support a pedophile made no sense. My anger grew as the stories unfolded. I wanted out.

But God was not quite ready to let me leave the Catholic Church. In my early 40s, I was attending a noon mass at a local church. I was alone (I'm beginning to see a pattern). The choir director, to whom I had never spoken, walked up to me out of the blue and asked me to sing in his choir. He did not know me, and certainly, he had never heard me sing. Two weeks later I was in a Catholic Church choir that I would enjoy for the next 10 years. It is difficult for me to share the story of joining the choir without emotion. There I was, trying to escape the Catholic Church and I was drawn back in. My choir director would tell the story differently, "Judy needed a choir and I needed an alto; everybody was happy."

Even though I loved my ministry, I still felt the need to leave the Catholic Church after constantly hearing about the sex crimes and cover-ups, but the joy of singing in the choir would tug me back. I became co-director of the youth choir. It was a beautiful experience. The music was superb and the choir family, even better. I loved working with the kids — the job came with angelic voices and hugs. My choir sang and prayed at both of my parents' funerals and their voices wrapped around me like a warm blanket, offering me comfort when I needed it most.

But over and over, I was forced to face the pedophilia that plagued the Catholic faith. Pray for the victims, pray for the priests, pray for the Catholic Church. It was getting more complex. My safe place had betrayed me. I wasn't a victim of the Catholic Church first hand, but every time another story is revealed, I am reminded of my own sexual abuse. The pain of the survivors is never acknowledged or validated properly: there are lawsuits and the victims are awarded and silenced. Religion is very personal and important to me. I am a believer although I no longer attend the Church where my faith began.

One day, I knew it was "time to pluck up that which is planted" and finally left the Catholic Church. In the course of one week, two different people from the church had raised their voices at me. Rather than resolve the issues, I determined it was a sign and decided to start anew. A few months earlier, my son asked if we could join a church where he had been invited by a friend to play basketball with the youth group. I took his lead and attended a service there. The choir sang "Come to the Water." It was a personal invitation, maybe even a special delivery.

We now are very active at that church, part of the Reformed Church of America. I still delight in the opportunity to praise God by singing in a choir. I enjoy the church community. And since being at the new church, I haven't once been reminded of my own sexual abuse. I can relax and enjoy my relationship with God. The anger and resentment I once felt dissipated because I am no longer asked to pray for the sick priests and their victims. Guilt is no longer associated with my sins. I trust the men and women in my new church.

Why didn't I make the change sooner? Perhaps for the same reasons I didn't tell of being molested in my youth. Perhaps I was worried about what others would think. Maybe I would disappoint my family and Catholic friends. As I see it, I shared my sexual abuse story 20 years too late. I could have left the Catholic Church sooner, but it wasn't yet my time to cast away.

JUDY FERRARO

My first professional photograph in my 20s. I'm on my way!

12 A LIFETIME OF "IFS"

With sexual abuse comes betrayal, initially by the predator. More often than not, it is someone the victim knows, likes, or even loves and trusts. When survivors conceal the abuse, we then begin to betray ourselves. Quite possibly we are betraying others who also become victims of the same pedophile. When and if survivors of sexual abuse decide to share our horrendous experiences, betrayal may step into play and rear its ugly head once again. This time, the betrayal comes from the people we trust enough to tell. When victims are not understood and supported — or worse — are accused of lying, it is the worst form of betrayal. Perhaps the abuse is best kept a secret to diminish the pain of telling.

Close family members have chosen to never discuss my sexual abuse with me. Perhaps they didn't believe me. Maybe it makes them uncomfortable. Whatever the reason is, unbeknownst to them, their lack of acknowledging my experience is a form of betrayal to me. I need to talk to them. Maybe they can still help me. Their choice is to ignore the experience so they can pretend it didn't happen. I could have chosen to go through life feeling like they didn't care. That's not the case. We abuse survivors get used to avoidance and denial. We know that those who love us are not trying to hurt us. We avoid the topic and, therefore, avoid the pain.

The "ifs" and consequences for concealing the abuse for all those years continue to haunt me. If I had told my mother sooner, maybe the abuse would have been stopped immediately.

If Terry hadn't come to live with us, would Gil have ever gotten to know my family so well?

If I had told Tammy about Gil's sexual advances, maybe sweet little Margaret would have been spared the horrific experience of being sexually molested by her mother's husband.

If I had told Gil's mother, maybe she would have been incensed that he had touched me, her little protégé, and punished him. His sickness would have been on the radar and maybe his own daughters would have been protected from his sexual advances, and the aftermath that follows.

If I hadn't been so confused sexually, I would have understood the difference between love and lust and made better relationship decisions.

If I had only known how to tell my first husband about my experience, maybe I wouldn't have left him so abruptly. Maybe he could have understood. Maybe I wouldn't have been so hurtful. He didn't deserve my behavior. I tried to make amends. He wasn't receptive.

I wish I had discussed my childhood experiences with my first husband's mother. She was so insightful. If I had, I'm sure she would have made certain that I received the therapy I needed. I never told her or anyone else because the thought of it all made me feel ashamed.

If I had shared my story right away, I could have gone to counseling sooner. I could have learned to forgive myself and maybe even Gil. He was sick. He needed help. I could have been the catalyst for that help, early on.

If the Catholic Church had only handled the sex crimes properly, maybe I would still be a Catholic.

I own a lifetime of "ifs." I can't seem to shake them. The "ifs" will always be there, but I have chosen to relinquish my anger and cling to the joys that fill my life.

My first boss, Ray, another good guy.

13 IN SPITE OF THE MOLESTATION

In spite of what had happened to me, I am a confident person and have created success in my life. Although there were horrific circumstances hurled in my direction, I managed to cope and prevail.

My parents never encouraged me to attend college. I was told they were saving to send their son to school. My mother encouraged me to be a secretary and that is exactly what I did.

I started attending college at night while during the day, I worked for a general agent at an insurance company. The company paid for my studies. As it turned out, working for this very talented general agent was like going to college for me. Every day his wisdom and knowledge poured into me. He transformed my understanding the sales process and what it takes to survive in business. I began to realize there was a career path in sales where I could use my strengths. I learned how to become a salesperson and got stronger and stronger.

I worked for 10 years as Ray's administrative assistant. He took me to seminars with speakers who inspired sales people to excel. I watched him coach and motivate his 20-person sales team. He hired the insurance company's second female and first African-American. He used to say, "If you know where you are going, any road will take you there." That quote still rings true for me.

I left that job with some college credits and tremendous sales knowledge. I was just divorced and I thought it best to start anew. I took a job working as an administrative assistant in downtown Chicago. My new boss was an urban guy and from him I learned about Chicago. Instead of only attending White Sox games, I started going to Bears, Bulls, Blackhawks and Cubs games. I learned what restaurants and bars were hip. I played softball in Olive Park next to Navy Pier and worked out at the prestigious East Bank Club. I started attending DePaul's College of Commerce. I was on the right track.

The biggest leap of my life was my first sales job in 1984. I was to buy scrap metal from manufacturers. I wasn't even sure what scrap metal meant. I was offered a sales job and I took it. I left my administrative assistant position where I was making over $25,000 a year and accepted the scrap metal buyer position at a base salary of $200 a week and a tank of gas. I was also offered commissions on everything I could buy. My parents thought I was crazy considering that my own father never made more than $35,000 in one year. But I took the job and never looked back.

I took to the scrap metal business like cream cheese to a bagel, loved the company I represented, and idolized my boss. I became successful in a short time. I made hundreds of cold calls every week. The numbers game was something I learned when attending seminars with Ray. I was grateful for the opportunity and finally free to control my own destiny. I loved every moment of my job. In the meantime, I kept attending DePaul.

By 1986, I was making over six figures, living in the city, and enjoying my new life. There were the usual ups and downs of relationships but I continued to move forward. I went on to own and operate my own scrap metal company for 10 years. This meant obtaining enough customers to sustain the salaries of a workforce of 10, putting up with 12-hour work days and enduring adversities such as dealing with the embezzlement of business funds by an employee and a fire that ruined our building and trucks.

I was fortunate to sell that business just before the markets and economy collapsed in 1999. Four years later, I created a consulting company to motivate and train sales teams which has blossomed into managing high-level projects and marketing endeavors in the recycling industry. I write a column called "On Sales" in Scrap Magazine for which I won an American Society of Business Publication Editors gold award.

These accomplishments have to do with believing in myself. Achieving success and being self-sufficient is empowering for me. And it's not over; I work on it every day. For me, success is a journey, not a destination.

I read repeatedly about the obstacles faced by those who have been sexually abused. Because I concealed my experience, the problems didn't exist for me — or so I believed. On the path to success, I wouldn't let the sadness control my destiny. I am driven. I learned from my mistakes, and I moved on. And throughout my entire life, I have been able to laugh and experience joy. It is the best medicine.

The proverbial spoon on the nose trick. This takes talent.

On stage at Second City.

My sense of humor never escaped me.

14 SENSE OF HUMOR

What does a sense of humor have to do with sexual abuse? For me, it was the steadfast positive in my life. It was a way of coping. It was a way of pulling me out of what seemed like a deep dark hole. As much as I discuss anger and pain in this book, it is important to talk about the happy times and my sense of humor.

Early on, I knew I was funny. I was the inquisitive kid in class with the obnoxious and constantly waving hand, looking to be called on, to ask or answer a question. I was talkative and flaunted my gift of gab. I found I could entertain people

with my stories about family, school, work, relationships —
even chasing perverts.

I recall a Saturday morning catechism class when I was 9
years old. The assignment was to write something we could
do every day that would show our love for God. I remember
writing, "I want to make at least one person smile every day
of my life." Others were contemplating the right answer,
which, of course, was to pray. I finished before them and sat
with a smirk on my face. I liked being done first; it made me
feel smarter than everyone else. Sister Mary Therese looked
over my shoulder and smiled. She said, "Consider this the
first day." From that moment on, it became a quest. I strive
to be positive and have the ability to find humor when others
choose to be irritated.

I'm sure if they had had a Class Clown Award in high
school, I would have been in contention. My teachers liked
me. I was clever and funny; the sparring was fun. My friends
could count on my wit. I have the ability to make people
smile. My gift, my quest.

In my late teens, I worked for my Uncle Bernie in the Old
Town neighborhood of Chicago where he owned
handwriting-analysis machines. The machines were a form of
entertainment. Passersby wrote their names on a key card
and the card sorter electronically punched the cards and spit
out a stack of bogus personality characteristics. When the

crowds diminished and if time allowed, I sneaked down the block and slipped into the back row of Second City improvisational theater to watch comedy's rising stars. John Belushi, Bill Murray and Betty Thomas parodied Chicago people and politics. There was no holding back. I was hooked. Second City became a place where I went to laugh. I wasn't aware that I could have been one of the players myself until early in my 30s.

I was dating a writer. Things didn't work out for us, but he did tell me, "You are very funny. Did you ever think about going to classes offered by improv groups around Chicago?" I followed up on his recommendation and signed up for Jo Forsberg's Player's Workshop and immediately became addicted to the high of making comedy. Our class ended with a graduation show at Second City. It was one of the highlights of my life. Then I started taking classes at Second City. The classes were like a drug for me. There is no downside to laughter.

After Second City, I took classes at Improv Olympic (now called IO) and was lucky enough to study under Del Close. Del was one of the original University of Chicago Compass Players, the first formal improv ensemble. He once said to me over dinner, "Ferraro, women just aren't funny, but you do make me smile at times." Bingo. After all, making people smile was my original holy goal.

Occasionally, I am asked to do a standup routine at local charity events so I'm always making notes of funny situations, just in case. I am elated for my improv classmates who have gone on to become famous writers, actors and directors. They are my brush with greatness.

Although my childhood was damaged by sexual abuse, my sense of humor never wavered in my life. It is my gift, and no one could take that from me, not even Gil.

15 TRIGGERS

While writing this book I met a woman for breakfast. She attended one of my motivational speaking engagements and we became fast friends. During our first conversation, she disclosed to me that she was a survivor of sexual abuse. I don't really know how or why she began to share her story with me, but there we were, practically strangers, discussing something as personal as sexual abuse. Speaking with someone who understands and has effectively pursued the healing process is extremely comforting. We get it; we have lived it.

Over the course of writing this book, I have had people reach out to assist me, cheer me on, share their secrets and give me consent to discuss them here. I connect with these women and men on many levels: spiritually, intellectually, emotionally and, of course, through our journeys of healing.

One of the women asked me an interesting question: "Where are you on the meter of being cured? What percentage would you say you are?" Her question caused me to pause. I had never rated my healing.

"I don't know if the abused, just like the abusers, can ever be cured," I replied. "If I had to chart the healing, I would say it is more like a graph, with lines spiking above and below the normal line, depending on the relentless barrage of triggers."

She nodded in agreement. "I find myself way over the top and not thinking about the abuse and then it all comes back," she said. Both of us were now nodding in agreement about how just the mere reference of sexual abuse — in the news, in a conversation, or even a movie — can drag us back into our dark abysses.

While writing this book, I scheduled a dinner with the friend who originally suggested I seek therapy for my sexual abuse. And there we were, a quarter of a century later, still sharing dinners. She asked me what I was up to and I told her I was writing a book about sexual abuse. Her eyes immediately filled with tears, her hands using the white restaurant napkin to wipe them away. She was uncomfortable and apologized. I felt responsible for sending her below the normal line. I had become her trigger. Damn!

Most of those who have shared their stories with me over the past couple of years had been sexually abused by a relative such as a father, a mother, a brother. Some encounter those relatives at family functions. They attend these events to keep peace or honor a parent. I would not be so compliant. I can't imagine the pain sexual abuse survivors must feel as they sit through a Thanksgiving dinner across the table from their abusers.

One survivor shared her abuse story with me. She had been penetrated as early as three years old. I felt lucky, once again, that I had not experienced penetration. I wondered if she felt that the sexual abuse I encountered wasn't all that bad in comparison. And there I was, graphing my experience, measuring my level of abuse against hers.

A late night viewing of an Oprah show with an audience of 200 men who had been sexually abused certainly set off my "healing meter." I'm not sure I could sit in a room filled with abuse survivors wondering about their lives and where they are in their journey. I hardly slept that night. My heart was heavy and filled with sadness. I didn't want to close my eyes because I feared I would be brought back to those terrible times in my own life.

Where we are on the healing meter affects the relationships around us every day of our lives. I find intimacy difficult on the days when my healing meter reading is below normal. In spite of the highs and lows, I am thankful for my full and abundant life. I have my faith, family and friends. I enjoy being my husband's wife and my greatest joy is being the mother of my son. I sing, I write, I have an eye for taking interesting photographs, and people tell me I am funny. They are correct. All are blessings.

Everything that is positive helps remind me that I am on the better side of healing. Being grateful for the blessings and embracing the joy that surrounds me are tremendous healers. Knowing how to recover from the negative is key. It is like beginning to fall and regaining balance before I hit the floor. I have become a pro at keeping myself upright. Knowing what makes me happy is useful. The negative spikes can be remedied simply by calling or texting a loved one who makes me laugh or watching my dog Maggie eat and enjoy red peppers. That's really not supposed to happen; dogs don't like red peppers. She does this to make me smile.

My healing meter reading is high right now. Sharing my story helps mend the wounds. I am hopeful that my journey will help others in their healing process. Perhaps my experience can provide information to parents and teachers of children whose hearts may be aching. And most important, this can help further my quest to encourage parents to speak to their children early and often. Their young bodies belong only to them and they must tell someone they trust — anyone — if they are approached in an inappropriate manner. Make them understand that no one will be mad. There is nothing to be ashamed of.

I encourage those who have been afflicted to find their way to the many therapy options available to abuse survivors. I have not spoken to a single abuse survivor who hasn't been to at least three different counselors, some as many as 13. I have seen three counselors, each with a different style, each who led me part of the way on my journey of healing.

There is no question that childhood abuse forms and reforms its victims. Abuse survivors who recognize they are on a journey know how to hang in there. There is a light at the end of the tunnel. We see and are attracted to the light. Unfortunately, the tunnel never ends. We are all right. There was once a time when the light did not exist.

JUDY FERRARO

EPILOGUE

THE PATERNO INFERNO

The triggers never stop. As this book neared completion, new tragic accounts of abuse invade the media. Like a wildfire raging out of control, the Penn State sexual abuse scandal was on every channel and newspaper for weeks. And even though Jerry Sandusky is in jail, the story will not go away anytime soon. Similar episodes from other team programs have surfaced. These accounts have a new and different impact since they are about men and boys.

I'll bet a paycheck that nine out of 10 males would change the channel rather than watch a story about a sexually abused girl. But now these stories are airing during sports events, the news and cable stations, on ESPN, and the Internet. Grown men cry over the very thought of their favorite coach or college concealing abominable crimes to save reputations.

In a conversation with my 17-year-old son about the Penn State abuse allegations, he said, "Sandusky is mentally ill, I know he did bad things, but what about all the people around him who concealed the whole scandal and are not mentally ill? Which party is worse?"

For the criminals and their abettors, it's all about image. If the secrets are divulged, what will it do to me? Our family? This institution? What will people think? Why put a child through painful questioning? This will rip apart our family (or athletic program, school, church, neighborhood — you name it.) But the survivor knows that the most painful part of the abuse is the secret they then must hold inside them, day and night. The pain worsens when the child gathers the courage to tell a trusted friend or family member and no action is taken. Or when this serious crime is not taken seriously. A friend eloquently described a child's telling of sexual abuse as "ringing the bell." She continued, "You can't "un-ring the bell. Once sounded, the victim must be heard."

Penn State's deceitful handling of its criminal situation reminds me again of the Catholic Church and of those who cover up sexual abuse. The bell rung has escalated to that of a gong. More stories are surfacing. I think the public will be astounded to learn of the widespread abuse and elaborate cover-ups in reputable places and families. Lawyers will profit and victims and families may be awarded settlements. But there is no amount of money that can end the physical and mental pain inflicted.

This is indeed a wildfire. There will come a day when the flames and smoke vanish, and the offenders and those guilty of concealment may be punished. But the embers will continue to smolder within the victims. Justice or no justice, it's what happens.

JUDY FERRARO

RESOURCES

RAPE and INCEST
1-800-656-HOPE
24 Hours/7 Days A Week
www.rainn.org
The Rape, Abuse & Incest National Network is the nation's largest anti-sexual assault organization. RAINN operates the National Sexual Assault Hotline at 1.800.656.HOPE and carries out programs to prevent sexual assault, help victims and ensure that rapists are brought to justice. Inside, you'll find statistics, counseling resources, prevention tips, news and more. National sexual assault hotline. Free. Confidential. 24/7.

Childhelp USA
1-800-422-4453
www.childhelp.org
A hotline staffed 24 hours a day, 7 days a week with professional crisis counselors who, through interpreters, can provide assistance in 170 languages. Offers crisis intervention, information, literature, and referrals to thousands of emergency, social service, and support resources. All calls are anonymous and confidential.

Darkness to Light
www.d2l.org
Organization with a mission to empower people to prevent child sexual abuse.

Erin's Law
www.erinslaw.org
Erin's Law requires that all public schools, in each state that passes it, implement a prevention-oriented child sexual abuse program.

National Children's Advocacy Center
www.nationalcac.org
The NCAC models, promotes, and delivers excellence in child abuse response and prevention through service, education and leadership.

Oprah Winfrey Website
www.oprah.com/packages/sexual-abuse-resource-center.html
Visit Oprah's site for information on prevention, general resources and male survivors.

Prevent Child Abuse America
www.preventchildabuse.org
Preventing the abuse and neglect of the nation's children and includes all forms of abuse and neglect, whether physical, sexual, educational, or emotional or peer-peer abuse.

Bureau of Justice Assistance
www.bja.gov/evaluation/program-corrections
Provides leadership and assistance to local criminal justice programs that improve and reinforce the nation's criminal justice system.

ILLINOIS

CACI (Child Advocacy Centers of Illinois)
www.childrensadvocacycentersofillinois.org

Illinois Sex Offender Information
www.isp.state.il.us/sor/contactsor.cfm

Prevent Child Abuse Illinois
www.preventchildabuseillinois.org.

JUDY FERRARO

TESTIMONIALS

I enjoyed reading *If I Catch You I Will Kill You* and believe it will help and encourage others to face their own toxic memories.

Tena Marsilio, survivor

One tough thing about being a police officer is never knowing if the child who disclosed to you that he or she has been sexually or physically abused turned out okay in the end. You can make them safe, get them moving in the direction of help, even arrest the person who has harmed them. But you never get to know if, down the road, that child is having the happy life that a criminal tried to steal away.

Judy's book gives me such hope that, like her, it is possible for those hurt kids to become strong, wise, healthy and even very humorous humans who lay claim to the life they deserve. Judy's story gave me hope. But more importantly, I believe it will provide hope to sexual abuse victims and their families.

Sgt. Therese Thompson, Lemont Police Dept., Lemont, IL

What a testimony to the resiliency of a survivor! It is so important to break the silence and make your personal political to empower other survivors. Judy's story gives another face to survivors of abuse: a face that is neither downcast nor crushed, but a face that is thriving.

Judy Ferraro has found her voice and with no apology tells her story of survival to empower other abuse survivors. She shows the reader that in despite lack of support from the systems that should protect, most survivors display incredible strength, empathy and resiliency as they move forward in their healing process. This life story will inspire every woman survivor who is trying to reclaim her life to not just survive, but thrive.

Dr. Denise Fraser Vaselakos, psychologist

Reading a good book is symbolic of a friendship: something you want to cherish and something you never want to end. I found myself towards the end of Judy's book forcing myself to read slowly. I did not want it to end—the sign of a great story. Her book will help others to find the courage to share their own stories so that they may begin to heal as well. Thank you for sharing your story with me and so many others.

Jennifer Samartano BSW, MS, child abuse prevention specialist

Judy's story will be helpful to the victims and survivors of sexual abuse. Her words will give encouragement to seek and find the means to tell and the strength to heal. In addition, it will assist probation officers, sex offender treatment providers, judges and others within the criminal justice system to enhance their education of the manipulative grooming by the offender and the devastating impact of child sexual abuse on the victims and survivors.

This traumatic and beautiful story is an affirmation to my commitment since 1991 when I founded an adult sex offender probation program and continuous devotion to its expansion. It is a program dedicated to providing sex offenders with new skills while holding them accountable to make behavior changes to assist in the prevention of future incidences of sexual abuse.

Judy validates the commitment and hope that our work will result in no more victims.

Sandra K. White, M.S., Probation Officer Supervisor
Adult Court Services Division, DuPage County, IL

I can't wait to share this book with other patients.

Dr. M. Sobel, psychologist who treated Judy

JUDY FERRARO

ACKNOWLEDGEMENTS

I don't know if I could have chosen a better person to coach me through the writing of this book than Joan Howard. When first asked to partner with me on this journey, Joan did so with trepidation. Soon she was asking me poignant questions that triggered memories and compelled me to forge ahead with my story. Her own writing talent and delicate encouragement led me to the right words. Her nurturing guidance, love and delightful home-cooked meals during the months and then years of writing this book will be memories to cherish. I have always loved and admired Joan and this book has only deepened my relationship with her.

Like mother, like daughter. Christina Koenig, Joan's daughter and my sister-like friend, made sure that the commas, dashes, capitalizations and words were just right. She questioned me into providing more detail and made writing a book about a grueling subject a fun project.

Thanks to Marie Carberry at SchrecDesign who created a beautiful cover.

Thank you Aidan Nicole Salon in Palos Park and special thanks to my good friend Lisa Henif for coordinating such a successful photo for the cover of this book.

So many of my friends and relatives read and reread this

book during the writing process, offering me punctuation, edits, questions and fortitude to allow my project to come to fruition. A special thanks to my niece Jene who listened as I read the book out loud to find the initial edits, and my sisters, Jean and Jeanette, who assisted me with the chronological and family information discussed in the book.

And last but not least, to my gentle husband Michael and loving son Eric who are the loves of my life. My devotion to you both is never ending.

ABOUT THE AUTHOR

Judy has achieved success in the recycling industry, as a comedian in Chicago's comedy scene, a sales trainer for professionals and a public speaker. She recently received a National Gold Award from the American Society of Business Publications Editors. She lives in suburban Chicago with her husband and son.

Judy would like to hear from you. You can write to her at:
judy@judyferraro.com.